*Cavafy's
Alexandria*

Cavafy's Alexandria

Study of a Myth in Progress

Edmund Keeley

Harvard University Press
Cambridge, Massachusetts
1976

HOUSTON PUBLIC LIBRARY

77-007593-5

R01 0222 2577

Copyright © 1976 by Edmund Keeley
All rights reserved
Printed in the United States of America
Library of Congress Cataloging in Publication Data
Keeley, Edmund.
    Cavafy's Alexandria.
    Bibliography: p.
    Includes index.
1. Kabaphēs, Kōnstantinos Petrou, 1863-1933.
2. Greeks in Egypt. I. Title.
PA5610.K2Z73   889'.1'32   76-6997
ISBN 0-674-10430-7

For Constantine Trypanis,
who first encouraged me to read Cavafy
during Michaelmas term, 1950

Acknowledgments

Working in Modern Greek literature is a lonely enterprise: few know its riches, very few teach the subject, even fewer come to the literature as scholars or critics, especially in the United States, where there is still, at this writing, no graduate course anywhere devoted to the study of Modern Greek texts in the original and no professorship of any kind in the field. I therefore recognize a more than normal gratitude for the help of those who have made my task here less lonely in various ways. George Savidis has given me easy access to his knowledge of Cavafy's work over many years; the leads he provided me in the early stages of my research for this book proved crucial, and as my several specific allusions to his scholarship indicate, he remained an essential source throughout, both in person and in print. Stratis Tsirkas, Robert Liddell, and Basil Athanassopoulos supplied valuable biographical information that guided my approach to Cavafy's literal city during a trip to Egypt in the spring of 1973, a trip made particularly memorable by the hospitality of Magdi and José Wahba and of Uncle Babi Nicolaidis. A number of colleagues and friends read portions of the manuscript at one stage or another and offered helpful suggestions: Peter Bien, Karen Kennerly, Carolyn Kizer, Peter Macridge, and Theodore Weiss. Cedric Whitman read the completed manuscript with his usual generosity and insight; his sensitive commentary led to an expansion of the concluding chapter. Robert Fagles' reading provided valuable assurance. Philip Sherrard did not read the manuscript, but his informal consideration of problems I raised on the shores of the Euboean Gulf gave new life to my thinking at the right time, as it has in the past. Several of my associates in the Modern Greek Studies Association and other casual Philhellenes were good enough to organize a hearing for sections of my work in progress at their home institutions: Apostolos Athanassakis, Harry Avery, Valerie Caires, John Dillon, Anne Farmakides, Frank Frost, John Hall, George Kennedy, Harry Levi, Lily Macrakis, Thanassis Maskaleris, Cary Woodward, and Charles Wright. I am also grateful to my students in Modern Greek 107 at Princeton who tolerated, no doubt at some expense of patience, my exploration of the main arguments of this study during the first four weeks of the course in the spring of 1975. Georges Borchardt helped to ensure that the manuscript found hospitable publishers and that the reader arrived at my argument with a proper introduction. D. J. Enright provided good advice before the manuscript became proof, and during the same period Harry Foster gave my text a thorough, careful reading that often made me rethink what I had written so as to eliminate ambiguities and syntactical eccentricities.

My work on this book was aided vitally at various times by a fellowship from the John Simon Guggenheim Memorial Foundation, by a leave of absence from Princeton, and by a grant from the University Research Committee in the Humanities and Social Sciences. Walter Kaiser, Alan Heimert, and Laura Gordon made possible a fruitful and amiable period of unencumbered concentration at Eliot House, Harvard, during the spring of 1974. Finally, I want to acknowledge with thanks those journals that published earlier versions of parts of this study in advance of publication here: *Boston University Journal, Shenandoah, The Southern Review* ("Cavafy's Metaphoric City"), and *Review of National Literatures* ("Cavafy's Hellenism" in the issue "Greece: The Modern Voice").

Edmund Keeley

Princeton, N.J.

Contents

chapter one

Introduction
The Literal City

Cavafy's "Exiles," one of his recently discovered "unpublished poems,"[1] places an exile from Constantinople in Arabic Alexandria during the reign of the Byzantine Emperor Basil I, A.D. 867-886.[2] The exile is making the best of what he hopes will be a short stay in a city that, while it still has its charms for the tourist, evidently is not the kind of cultural setting likely to satisfy a ninth-century Constaninopolitan more than briefly. The poem's speaker tries to be generous toward Alexandria ("Whatever war-damage it's suffered, / however much smaller it's become, / it's still a wonderful city"), but his tone betrays him throughout the poem, and it becomes clear by the end that he simply can't wait to get back home where the real action, not to mention the main chance, hovers before him in a future he takes very much for granted. Cavafy's ironic attitude toward this rather supercilious visitor to the center of his poetic universe is reinforced implicitly by the poem's historical context: it seems that our exile, who tells us that his stay in Alexandria "isn't unpleasant because, naturally, / it's not going to last forever," is very likely doomed to spend the rest of his life in this city he finds so moderately tolerable. The emperor who had to be overthrown before the exile could return to his own country actually kept his throne for twenty years and died peacefully in bed.

The historical moment depicted in "Exiles" falls about a thousand years after the brightest period of Ptolemaic Alexandria and another thousand years before Cavafy's birth on the Rue Cherif Pacha, when the Greek community of Alexandria was at its modern high point. In short, the Alexandria that our exile sees, though roughly midway through its 2200-year history, may not be exhibiting its richest possibilities for those devoted to the Greek way of life. But as the exile himself says in the opening line of his monologue, without fully comprehending the point, "Alexandria goes on being Alexandria still" for those who see it for what it really is—a city of the imagination, a city that satisfies the mind's eye first of all. Cavafy's irony mocks those who are blind to this insight regarding the Alexandria he came to love.

Aware of the poet's point of view, I find it difficult to move through the streets of today's Alexandria without feeling the presence of Cavafy's ghost, especially the threat of its mockery.

During a recent visit there, in the spring of 1973, I tried to make myself believe that the ugly reality I was seeing masked the presence of another city, more real in its way, a city open to those who could bring to it an imaginative vision, a mythical sensibility if you will, akin to Cavafy's and exemplified in recent English letters by E. M. Forster and Lawrence Durrell.[3] But the mask, the surface reality, was so unlike the literary images I brought with me, so immediate and harsh in its effect, that it frustrated any imaginative projection. Today's Alexandria strikes one first of all as squalid. If you walk along the esplanade leading to where the wondrous ancient Pharos used to stand (now Fort Kayet Bey, grotesquely restored as a museum celebrating the Egyptian navy), you will encounter odors and sights that will amaze you—if none of the palaces and monuments that amazed Cavafy's exiles. The wall at your side rises just high enough to block all by the most cunning attempts to find the sea beyond, but not high enough to conceal the spread of laundry-bannered tenements along the harbor's curve ahead. And the smells you breathe, cut only sporadically by a pinch of sea-salt, are of refuse not quite ripe enough to pass for garbage and urine a bit too spotty for official concern. The principal monuments in that part of town—the statues of Sa'ad Zaghlul and Mohammed Ali—are surrounded by open space that is quartered, apparently deliberately, into dirt plots blooming with weeds, trash, and broken glass. The broad concrete steps leading the visitor to a close-up view of these nineteenth-century heroes become precarious in the dusty patchwork of discarded cabbage leaves and fruit peelings. The city that spreads out from the esplanade has a surface perhaps less surprising, because all conflict between illusion and reality vanishes in the filth and stench of narrow unwashed streets overflowing with the murky drift of the poor, pushed on by pyjama-clad hawkers and ambitious urchins.

There is still a contemporary equivalent to our exile's "straight road ending at the Hippodrome"—the broad, tree-lined El Hurriya Avenue (formerly Rue Rosette, where Cavafy lived with his brother for a short time)—but it is now a sorry anachronism. Its modern palaces—homes for the established members of the foreign colony that brought much exploitation and snobbery, some progress, and a strong cosmopolitan flavor to Alex-

Cavafy's Alexandria

andria from the mid-nineteenth century until Gamal Abdel Nasser gave Egypt back to the Egyptians—are now shuttered tight with no outward sign of expectation, or they are awkwardly in service as quarters for the local bureaucracy. Lesser homes have been converted into tenements to carry the burden of immigration from outlying villages, and their facades are cracked and scorched from the effort.

Cavafy's last residence, a second-floor apartment with a balcony in what must once have been a rather impressive building, has now become the Pension Amir, each room a dormitory crammed with sway-backed beds and peeling wardrobes, the halls and staircase seemingly a World War II film set fashioned out of crude materials at hand to imitate the ravages brought on by guerrilla warfare in quarters occupied by an unfeeling enemy. The streets in that neighborhood, once alive with private enterprise, including an ample share of brothels, are now lined by garages and government-controlled stores. Even the name of the poet's street has been changed, from Rue Lepsius to Rue Sharm el Sheikh to commemorate the town on the Red Sea lost to Israel in the Six-Day War of 1967. The cafés that Cavafy frequented on the Rue Misalla (now Safiya Zaghlul) have been largely replaced by cheap shops, though one of his favorites, the Billiard Palace, is still there, now literally living up to its name. The most authentic Cavafian relic is an essentially metaphoric one: the dying Association Hellénique Eschyle-Arion, where "some of the very few . . . Greeks / still left in the city" (as the speaker in "Exiles" puts it) occasionally meet to play cards, hear a lecture, talk of the latest disaster to befall one of their number, and somehow pass the time until the gods find a way to help them escape to Greece, where they can look forward to the expatriation and nostalgia that seem inevitably to haunt those exiles from the Hellenic world who are doomed to a new life in the mother country.

The surface of Alexandria is now Arabic once again—Arabic and little else—and the mythical city beyond it is visible only to the inner eye of an Egyptian poet, one who can see the vital imaginative resources that remain hidden from those confined to a European perspective. But if the surface one sees today is unrecognizable to someone brought up on the images created by

Cavafy, Forster, and the other literary "Alexandrians," this merely serves to reinforce the sense that the literal Alexandria is not the one that has counted most for the world of letters. The mystery of modern Alexandria seems to be not in what it actually is or was at any given moment but in its power to stimulate—as perhaps no other city in this century—the creation of poetic cities cast in its image, cities that imitate it as it can be, or even ought to be, in its essence. It is in part this godlike attribute of Alexandria that Cavafy had in mind in "The God Abandons Antony," when he cunningly replaced Plutarch's Dionysus and Shakespeare's Hercules by the city itself as the god that abandoned Antony in his moment of ultimate defeat after Actium, the god's departure signaled by the sudden passing of an invisible procession of musicians. The poem suggests that Alexandria has always had a godlike power to move the mind of mortals with poetic conceptions of itself, at least in those the city finds worthy to receive this divine gift—a gift that can be withdrawn as well as granted:

As one long prepared, and full of courage,
as is right for you who were given this kind of city,
go firmly to the window
and listen with deep emotion
but not with the whining, the pleas of a coward;
listen—your final pleasure—to the voices,
to the exquisite music of that strange procession,
and say goodbye to her, to the Alexandria you are losing.

What one might call the Alexandrian mode is first of all to search for the hidden metaphoric possibilities, the mysterious invisible processions, of the reality one sees in the literal city outside one's window. If one is Cavafy, the mode is then to dramatize and expand these discovered possibilities until they carry a broad mythic significance. Cavafy's use of the mode begins with his choosing to move from personal metaphors to communal and historical metaphors, and from there to the projection of a self-contained mythical world that serves to represent both his special view of Greek history and his image of the perennial human predicament. A number of twentieth century writers have practiced a related mode, using a particular history or culture to project their own mythical cities. Cavafy offers perhaps the most accessible and precise model for this practice, certainly among the writers who used Alexandria. His model not only illustrates the development of an important poetic imagination but tells us something about the creative process that prevailed early in this century, when Yeats, Joyce, Pound, and Eliot (to name those in the English tradition) were shaping their individual myths out of the cities and countries of their imaginations.

Cavafy was the first of these to project a coherent poetic image of the mythical city that shaped his vision, and he did so while working very much on his own, after years of undistinguished effort in less fruitful modes. As George Seferis has pointed out, Cavafy wrote poems into his early thirties "with all signs showing that he [was] unable to produce anything of importance."[4] Then he began to find his mature voice, though it took him until his late forties to conceive the proper mythical structure for this voice. His development of the Alexandrian myth continued through his last years. Given his personal circumstances and his cultural milieu during his early and middle years, it is perhaps not surprising that he progressed slowly. In fact, some might see it as a measure of his genius, and of his intense inner commitment in the face of more than normal obstacles, that he was finally able to create work as consistently original as his mature poems.

Cavafy was born into a family that had been among the leading commercial families in the Greek community of Alexandria, but his father died when he was seven, leaving an inadequate inheritance, which was, in any case, soon dissipated by what the poet called the "unhappy speculations" of his older brothers.[5] His formative years were marked by poverty and dislocation. The available record shows only one year of formal schooling, at the Hermes Lyceum in Alexandria (a commercial school), though Cavafy may have attended a secondary school in England during his seven years there, between the ages of nine and sixteen, and he apparently read fairly widely during this period, and more especially during his three years in Constantinople, between the ages of nineteen and twenty-two. He returned to

Alexandria at twenty-two to spend the rest of his life in the same "small corner" of the world (as he puts it in "The City"), and though he continued to take part in the social life of the established Greek community, and though he remained keenly aware of having been born a rich man's son, his poverty and, perhaps more important, his homosexuality inevitably made him to some degree an outsider.

There is evidence that Cavafy often found the Alexandria of his youth oppressive (see chapter 2). The prejudices of his local community required him to hide his homosexual proclivities, and he seems to have found release only furtively in the bisexual brothels and casual encounters of the Quartier Attarine, late at night, having bribed a servant to conceal his tracks from his mother, Haricleia, with whom he lived until her death in 1899, when he was thirty-six. Though Cavafy's family, especially his "poet" brother John, was apparently sympathetic toward his literary aspirations, he had little guidance during his early development. Cavafy first met a distinguished author (Gregory Xenopoulos) at the age of thirty-eight, during one of his few trips to Athens, and it was not until the time of the First World War, when he was already past fifty, that he had an opportunity to be "constantly associated with his intellectual equals," as Robert Liddell put it.[6] He first began earning a regular salary at the age of twenty-nine, as a clerk in the Irrigation Service, copying reports, checking accounts, handling foreign correspondence, and translating documents (he was fluent in Greek, English, and French), an appointment he held for thirty years. He supplemented his salary by speculative earnings on the Egyptian stock exchange. These sources provided for a frugal life with a fluctuating income, though he was apparently never in desperate need; and if his work for the Irrigation Service was generally tedious, at least it left his afternoons free.[7]

Cavafy's early and middle life in Alexandria was clearly restricted and more than normally undramatic: partly *mondain*, partly secret, limited in literary and intellectual associations, evidently devoid of long-standing emotional relationships except within the circle of his family (his relationship with his heir, Alexander Singopoulos, began during the war years), publicly undistinguished, financially sparing when not precarious, gener-

Cavafy's Alexandria

ally unrewarding except in private ways. But his early literary isolation and his meager recognition were not entirely detrimental to his poetic progress, as he himself acknowledged. In 1907 he offered a revealing comment on the general indifference to literature in the modern Greek world and the difficulties this indifference created for the writer:

But side by side with all that is disagreeable and harmful in the situation, which becomes felt every day, let me note—as a piece of comfort in our woes—an advantage. The advantage is the intellectual independence which it grants. When the writer knows pretty well that only very few volumes of his edition will be bought . . . he obtains a great freedom in his creative work. The writer who has in view the certainty, or at least the possibility of selling all his edition, and perhaps subsequent editions, is sometimes influenced by their future sale . . . . almost without meaning to, almost without realizing—there will be moments when, knowing how the public thinks and what it likes and what it will buy, he will make some little sacrifices—he will phrase this bit differently, and leave out that. And there is nothing more destructive for Art (I tremble at the mere thought of it) then that this bit should be differently phrased or that bit omitted.[8]

Cavafy was so hungry for intellectual independence and the freedom to be gained by remaining an essentially private poet that he never offered a volume of his work for sale during his lifetime. In fact, he never really published his poems at all, in the ordinary sense. During his early and middle years, he not only severely restricted the audience for his poems but released only a small sample of what he had created while reaching his late maturity. As is indicated in the introduction to *Passions and Ancient Days* (p. ix), "between 1891 and 1904 he published only six poems out of the 180-odd that he wrote or rewrote during this period, the 'publication' consisting of broadsheets or pamphlets printed on order for distribution exclusively to his few friends and relatives." He issued his first pamphlet in 1904, when he was forty-one, a privately printed selection of fourteen poems in one hundred copies, "a sort of free sampler for those who might care to try his poetry" (p. x). And the pamphlet that followed, in 1910, contained only twenty-one of the 220-odd poems that he had written by that date, the edition again private and limited. Thereafter, his method of disseminating his work, along with periodical publication, was through increasingly heavy folders containing broadsheets and offprints, the folders kept up-to-date year after year by Cavafy himself and distributed by his own hand to his select audience of readers, sometimes with late revisions inserted by pen. Though the burden these folders eventually had to bear was relieved on several occasions by the poet's withdrawing some of the earlier broadsheets to be sewn into booklets, Cavafy died without having published a collected edition of his work and without having left definite instructions for one.[9]

This pattern of "publication" suggests not only "an uncommon aesthetic asceticism" (as the translators of *Passions and Ancient Days* put it)—a disdain for the marketplace and a commitment to the craft of poetry first of all—but also that Cavafy thought of his mature poems as a continuing, lifelong work with a particular unity, shaped from year to year yet remaining subject to his ordering imagination from beginning to end, an end that had not been fully realized at his death. It suggests too a confidence in ultimate recognition, whatever the contemporary climate may have been. And the climate began to change about the time the poet wrote his defense of intellectual independence; by 1907, the limited selection of his work that he had promulgated had started to attract attention in Alexandria, and to a lesser extent in Athens. He was taken up in that year by the circle of young Alexandrian literati called *Nea Zoe* (New Life), and poems by him were subsequently featured in the journal published by this group and also in the second important literary journal of the period, *Grammata*.

As we shall see, the years 1907 to 1911 appear to have been especially significant in shaping Cavafy's positive attitude toward his home city and in freeing him to make the best poetic use of both its present and its past. But neither his adjustment to Alexandria nor his growing recognition there exerted a strong influence on the pattern of either his private life or his writing life. Though he sometimes received the local literati in his home and though he established several influential literary relationships within the foreign community during the war years—most notably with E. M. Forster—he lived alone in his apartment on Rue Lepsius throughout the last twenty-five years of his life, the period of his greatest enterprise, during which he wrote most of the poems that became the Cavafy "canon."[10] As his local reputation grew, he was apparently not above a certain self-advertisement in his corner of the world, but as Robert Liddell writes, he seemed "to have little interest in his reputation abroad."[11] In any case, he got little recognition even in Athens until the very end of his career, though the Greek dictator Pangalos awarded him the Order of the Phoenix in 1926 and though he was appointed to the international committee for the Rupert Brooke memorial statue on Skyros in 1930—rather meager returns for a poet of his accomplishment.

This failure to achieve a just place in Greek letters during his lifetime does not mean that Cavafy himself was indifferent to the progress of poetry in mainland Greece; on the contrary, he was often ironic about it, especially about the ascendancy of Kostis Palamas, the leading Greek man of letters during Cavafy's mature years, a prolific poet who played a crucial role in the development of modern Greek literature but who worked in a rhetorical mode very different from Cavafy's (the Alexandrian is reported to have distinguished between his good whisky and his second-rate "Palamas whisky" when deciding what to offer writers and artists visiting his apartment).[12] Again, Cavafy seems to have been confident that the mode he had developed would not only survive the test of time, however unpropitious the literary climate during his day, but that it would come to dominate Greek letters in due course. Now, some forty years after his death, the influence of his work, not only in Greece but in the English-speaking world as well, appears to be bearing him out.

We have seen that Cavafy began slowly and reticently, and that he rejected much of his early work with just harshness;[13] but what is more important, once he discovered the proper avenue for his talent, he still continued to develop, and he did so with a rigor and at the same time an assurance that were nourished by the intellectual independence he so jealously courted. The development is manifest, first of all, in a progress from subjective to increasingly objective representation, from didactic expression to subtle dramatization, and, in those poems set in contemporary Alexandria, from a general and sometimes vague treatment of erotic themes to a detailed delineation of specific figures, settings, and encounters. The latter poems also progress from an implicit to an explicit representation of homosexual eroticism, an advance that is not so much a development in artistic subtlety and range as a calculated program of revelation. But the most important development—that which serves best to demonstrate Cavafy's originality—is manifest in the central mythic structure that he created, a progress that can be plotted against the chronology of his work both before and after 1911, the year he himself apparently chose to herald his poetic maturity.[14] (See chapter 2, note 2, and the chronological tables in the appendix.) The chapters of this book reflect what I take to be the major stages of his development in this regard: from an early preoccupation with cities as personal and communal metaphors, to the creation of the mythical city at the center of his mature work—a poetic evocation of Alexandria in both its contemporary and ancient manifestations—and from this to a preoccupation with other mythical cities of the Hellenistic empire —Antioch, Selefkia, Sidon, Beirut—a preoccupation that broadened in his later years to include Sparta and Byzantium, allowing Cavafy to project a view of Greek history across eighteen centuries. Cavafy's perspective thus came to embrace almost the full world of Hellenism and to move beyond his image of the Alexandrian sensibility to a survey of the Greek experience in general. And in his very last poems we find his perspective reaching out toward a still more universal image of the human predicament, one that expresses his tragic sense of life in both ideological and historical terms, yet without pedantry, chauvinism, or bias.

My purpose in the chapters that follow is to trace the poet's aesthetic development, as he perfected his mature voice, and to delineate the expanding contours of his central myth. In this way I hope to approach a definition of the continuing "work in progress" that Cavafy's mature poems constituted—as George Seferis was the first to see[15]—a definition that may serve to illustrate the particular quality of his achievement and its relevance to contemporary experience.

Cavafy's Alexandria

chapter two

The Metaphoric City

When Cavafy arranged the contents of his first bound booklet of poems in 1917, the poem he chose to head the small selection he included was "The City," a choice that suggests the emphasis he wished to give to an image that had become, by that date, the central one in his work.[1] What we have in "The City," originally written in 1894 but first published in April 1910, is an Alexandria without name, history, or precise definition, and in this sense the most primitive and least developed version of an image that began to take full shape late in the year "The City" appeared.[2] But the poem is important as an index of the poet's method and intention—even, perhaps, of his personal commitment—at a crucial point in his artistic development.

You said: "I'll go to another country, go to another shore,
find another city better than this one.
Whatever I try to do is fated to turn out wrong
and my heart lies buried like something dead.
How long can I let my mind moulder in this place?
Wherever I turn, wherever I look,
I see the black ruins of my life, here,
where I've spent so many years, wasted them, destroyed them
    totally."
You won't find a new country, won't find another shore.
This city will always pursue you.
You'll walk the same streets, grow old
in the same neighborhoods, turn gray in these same houses.
You'll always end up in this city. Don't hope for things else-
    where:
there's no ship for you, there's no road.
Now that you've wasted your life here, in this small corner,
you've destroyed it everywhere in the world.

If one considers this poem in isolation—that is, outside the context of what Cavafy was writing not only during the sixteen years between the first draft of the poem and its publication in 1910 but also in the years immediately following—it is easy to take it as merely a heightened statement of mood, even of personal predicament,[3] in the manner of other early Cavafy poems, though given a degree of vitality by the dialogue form and the expanded metaphor that dominates the second stanza. Cavafy's often quoted comment on the earliest version of the poem, contained in a letter written (in English) to Pericles Anastasiadis not long after the first draft was written, would seem to sustain this reading of the published version:

"In the Same City" is from one point of view perfect. The versification and chiefly the rhymes are faultless. Out of the 7 rhymes on which this poem is built, 3 are identical in sound and 1 has the accent on the antepenultimate. But I have "parakamei" [overdone] it and somehow got cramped on the exigencies of the meter; and I am afraid I haven't put in the second stanza as much as I should have got into it. I am not sure that I have drawn in the 2nd, 3rd, and 4th lines of the second stanza an adequately powerful image of ennui—as my purpose was. It may be however that by trying to do more, I should have overdone the effect and strained the sentiment, both fatal accidents in art. There is a class of poems whose role is "suggestif." My poem comes under that head. To a sympathetic reader—sympathetic by culture— who will think over the poem for a minute or two, my lines, I am convinced, will suggest an image of the deep, the endless "desperance" which they contain "yet cannot all reveal."[4]*

The intention of the draft, as the letter suggests, is to present an image of a state of mind, of the "ennui" that was represented in other poems of this period, such as "Monotony" (1898),[5] and of the partially hidden "desperance" found in "Walls" (1896) and "The Windows" (1897). The fatal accidents to be feared are those of exaggerated effect and strained sentiment. The poem is intended to suggest a mood that cannot be fully revealed. This intention is still apparent in the published version offered some

*As the poet's commentary here suggests, Cavafy was interested in formal experimentation during the early stages of his development—in fact, obviously proud of his dexterity as a rhymer—and though he came to prefer a kind of free verse for the majority of his dramatic and narrative poems, and though his use of rhyme became casual in the late years, he never ceased to rhyme for emphasis or irony or lyrical effect, and he continued to write poems in more or less strict syllabics to the end of his career. The period that concerns us in this chapter was the period of Cavafy's greatest enthusiasm for strict forms, the number of rhymed poems slightly exceeding those not rhymed, the rhyme schemes often tight and occasionally elaborate, the rhymes frequently homophonous, and the unrhymed poems usually following strict syllabic patterns, these varying between eleven and sixteen syllable lines. Yet the best poems of the pre-1911 period—"Thermopylae," "Waiting for the Barbarians," "Trojans," "The Footsteps," "The Satrapy," and "The Ides of March"—though governed by fairly regular metrics, are all unrhymed. After 1911, the rhymed poems are fewer in number than those that are unrhymed, and the rhyme schemes become increasingly loose. Most of the more familiar historical-mythical poems and almost all of the longer

Cavafy's Alexandria

fifteen years after these remarks were made, but the revised text does serve to qualify it in illuminating ways. The revisions, as Stratis Tsirkas has pointed out,[6] though apparently minimal, reflect the poet's fears of exaggerated effect and strained sentiment: "Whatever I try to do is fated to turn out wrong" replaces "I'm disgusted by what my eye sees, by what my ear hears," and even more significantly, "Wherever I turn, wherever I look, / I see the black ruins of my life, here . . ." replaces "I hate the people here and they hate me, / here where I've spent half my life. . . ." But these revisions do not simply improve the poem aesthetically by muting hyperbolic or excessively personal sentiment; they depersonalize the image of the city and bring it more sharply into focus as the central metaphor of the poem. The same is true of the major revision in the second stanza: the substitution of "You'll always end up in this city. Don't hope for things elsewhere: / there's no ship for you, there's no road" for the early lines "However far you go, as far as you can possibly hope, / I will still see you in the same city."

By 1910 the poet's ambition seems to have become something larger than the effective suggestion of a mood, and the image he wishes to project is not simply that of personal "ennui" or "desperance" but of the soul's landscape in those confined inescapably by their own failure. The sentiments in the later version are presented not so much through bald subjective statement ("I hate the people here and they hate me") as through analogy to the

---

dramatic monologues and narrations make use of rhyme sporadically if at all, and the verse in these, though dominated by five and six-beat lines in terms of accentual pattern (normally not considered relevant in modern Greek prosody), become increasingly varied in their syllabic patterns. The poet's continuing interest in the more formal use of rhyme and meter becomes manifest in a new form that emerges in 1920 with "To Call up the Shades" (though anticipated by "He Swears," pub. 1915, and "In the Month of Athyr," pub. 1917): poems of varying length and stanzaic pattern that consist of lines that are typographically divided in two, the parts alternating between six and seven syllables and rhyming both internally and externally according to the poet's impulse, most often loosely, sometimes simply through the repetition of a word or phrase, and occasionally not rhyming at all. Sixteen poems assume this highly flexible form in some shape during the late years, though no one of these is among the very best of Cavafy's mature works. For specific details regarding the form of individual poems, the reader who has no Greek should consult Savidis' notes on rhyme and meter in *Collected Poems*.

persona's physical surroundings, which become, during the course of the poem, not the cause but the objective emblem of his state of mind: the black ruins that he sees wherever he looks in the altered first stanza, and the absence of a ship or road that might take him out of his predicament in the altered second stanza. The addition of the phrase "Don't hope for things elsewhere" also serves to raise personal sentiment and mood to a more general and symbolic level somewhat akin to that achieved by the ending of "Ithaka" (rewritten in the year this poem was published), where the poet tells his Ulysses figure that he will finally come to see, by making the very most of his long journey, "what these Ithakas mean." Here the phrase "things elsewhere" comes to represent the land of hope that will always remain beyond the reach of those trapped by the ruined city they have made out of their lives, and unnamed Alexandria, "this small corner" with its full possibilities for ennui, is finally exonerated by the implication of the metaphor, namely, that the city is only what you yourself make it.[7]

The poet's choice of "The City" as the lead poem of his thematic selections and the implications that emerge from a comparison of the early and late drafts of the poem suggest that he came to see this particular work as a kind of turning point or, more precisely, a culmination that might signal a new beginning. The culmination has reference to both a personal and an aesthetic history, which finally merge in the metaphor that concerns us here. On the personal side, we have both internal and external evidence that it took Cavafy some years to come to terms with the city he chose to live in continuously after 1885—that is, from the age of twenty-two until the age of seventy—and he seems to have resolved his feelings about Alexandria only shortly before he revised "The City" for publication. Cavafy's earliest recorded comment about Alexandria is that quoted by his friend Mikes Rallis in a letter written in 1883, answering one the twenty-year-old poet had sent him from Constantinople. Rallis writes: "When you claim that you hate Alexandria and 'all this futility', I don't believe you."[8] But since the poet had spent only some childhood and adolescent years in Alexandria at the time of this correspondence, it is not very illuminating for our purposes except as the first sign of what seems to have become a persistent ambivalence in his attitude toward the city, the product of a prospering love-hate relationship. The indirect internal evidence of the 1894 draft, "In the same City," with its "I hate the people here and they hate me, / here where I've lived half my life," seems more to the point because the poet had close to a decade of mature experience in Alexandria (if not quite half a lifetime) to give substance to his persona's rather less-than-ambivalent attitude. But the clearest evidence of persistent tension is an unpublished note dated thirteen years later (April 28, 1907), when the poet was forty-four years old:

> By now I've gotten used to Alexandria, and it's very likely that even if I were rich I'd stay here. But in spite of this, how the place disturbs me. What trouble, what a burden small cities are—what lack of freedom.
> I'd stay here (then again I'm not entirely certain that I'd stay) because it is like a native country for me, because it is related to my life's memories.
> But how much a man like me—so different—needs a large city.
> London, let's say. Since . . . P.M. left, how very much it is on my mind. [9]

This note tells us as much as we need to know. "By now I've gotten used to Alexandria" implies a long history of necessary adjustment that has now reached some resolution. Yet the burden of small cities—in particular the lack of freedom for "a man like me—so different"—persists even in the poet's forty-fourth year, during the third decade of his love-hate relationship with his "small corner" of the world. And the adjustment, the resolution, is still not complete at this time. Though the city has by now become a kind of native country for the poet, the home of his essential memories (and therefore the principal source of his erotic inspiration), he is still "not entirely certain" that he would stay in Alexandria were he rich enough to live elsewhere. The note ends with the poet turning toward a new land of hope, a larger city, perhaps better than this one: "London, let's say." And even if the general tone of the note, for all its fluctuations and qualifications, convinces us that the poet has no real intention of leaving his small corner of the world for a better city, the impulse of the first stanza of the 1894 draft is still with him thirteen years after it was written.

It is in the light of this history that his decision to revise and publish "The City" in 1910 assumes the status of a turning point, especially with the new emphasis that he gives his second stanza: "Don't hope for things elsewhere: / there's no ship for you, there's no road." Sometime during the three years between the 1907 note and the publication of his revised draft of the poem, Cavafy seems to have settled the question in his own mind once and for all. The implication of the revised draft is that the poet exonerates the city itself of blame for the predicament of his protagonist; the city is no longer seen as a cause of the predicament but as a metaphor for it. Depersonalized in this way, relieved of subjective motivation, the metaphoric city can now become a poetic image capable of subtle artistic exploitation. And since Alexandria is now free to assume the role of a vital poetic source, one that can be made to serve both "those sensual images" of the poet's contemporary Alexandria and his central "historical" myth, it can perhaps be accommodated fully in personal terms. Or, because it had been fully accommodated in personal terms, it could now take on its appropriate artistic role. Whichever came first, the poet's biography shows us that he moved into his new residence on Rue Lepsius in 1907 with his brother Paul and apparently was content to live there for the remaining twenty-six years of his life.[10] From 1910 on, he lived there by himself, not as a recluse, but as a man of letters increasingly devoted to his poetry. By 1911 he had ceased to write confessional entries in his diary and soul-searching notes of the kind quoted above. And it was at this time that he began to distribute his work to a select audience in folders of clipped off-prints and broadsheets, the contents kept continually up-to-date.[11]

It was also during 1910-11 that Cavafy apparently engaged in a thorough reevaluation of the poetry he had written to that date, choosing very little of his early work for continued circulation and designating the date 1911 to locate the beginning of his creative maturity.[12] George Savidis has suggested (in an unpublished lecture) that the year 1911 seems to mark the final stage of progress in the poet's changing conception of himself: from a gifted aesthete in search of his voice to a committed poet who knows where he is heading and who plans to devote himself diligently to getting there. I think we can now add that the poet's

Cavafy's Alexandria

accommodation with Alexandria, which included a recognition of the rich resources in ambiance, historical context, and mode that it could make available to him, not only proved crucial to his progress in this regard but influenced the particular course that his work took from 1911 onward.

The evidence for this contention does not rest solely on the 1910 version of "The City." The poem that was consistently second to it in each of Cavafy's thematic selections, "The Satrapy," carries similar implications, and this poem also appeared in print for the first time in 1910. The protagonist addressed in "The Satrapy" decides, in effect, to take the road that the speaker in the second stanza of "The City" warned did not exist. The road taken leads to Susa and the court of King Artaxerxes, a land of hope which, with all its "satrapies and things like that," can never satisfy the "you" of the poem, who is fated to discover, to his despair, that he goes on longing for what he can realize only in the city he left behind:

praise from the Demos and the Sophists,
that hard-won, that priceless acclaim—
the Agora, the Theatre, the Crowns of Laurel.

It is not specifically Alexandria that haunts the protagonist in this poem, nor is it the small, unnamed corner of the world that tormented the protagonist of "The City." But the concluding implications in the two poems are much the same: you won't find what you're looking for in "things elsewhere" (or, to use the language of this poem, "You can't get any of these from Artaxerxes, / you'll never find any of these in the satrapy") because the only life you can really live is in the city that your fate has already given you to know—in this case a city that holds within it not the black ruins of a life doomed to the same inner landscape through old age, but more positive images of possibility, that is, the "Crowns of Laurel" still open to those "cut out . . . / for grand and noble acts" who, however frustrated they may feel in their home city, do not give in to the temptations that the road to Susa symbolizes.

If we accept G. Lechonitis' commentary on "The Satrapy" as a reflection of Cavafy's attitude, then the personal reference of the poem becomes more precise.[13] Lechonitis tells us that the protagonist should not necessarily be taken as a political figure, such as Themistocles or Dimaratos, but "rather as an artist or even a scientist who, after knowing failure and disillusionment, abandons his art and takes the road to Susa" only to discover that this way out doesn't satisfy him. The implication, according to Lechonitis, is that the protagonist lost heart too easily, exaggerated his circumstances, and hurried his decision to take the road to Susa—an implication supported by the lines "And how terrible the day you give in / (the day you let go and give in), / and take the road for Susa." As Stratis Tsirkas has pointed out,[14] the circumstances of Cavafy's own poetic career in Alexandria changed significantly between 1907 and 1910—the date "The Satrapy" was published—enough so, perhaps, to explain why he chose to publish the poem in that year and subsequently to place it next to "The City" at the head of his thematic selections. After 1907 Cavafy began to receive enough recognition in his home city to make him an established man of letters. In particular, during 1908 Pavlos Petridis gave what George Savidis has called the first important lecture given on the poet, one that included a large sample of Cavafy's work to that date and that was subsequently published in *Nea Zoe*, a journal produced by the most active members of the younger generation of Alexandrian intellectuals. From this date forward, *Nea Zoe* generally opened its issues with a poem by Cavafy, and after 1910, other poems came out in the second influential journal that appeared in Alexandria at this time, *Grammata*. In short, after some years of frustration, Cavafy had begun by 1908 to gather in his small share of the "hard-won acclaim" and the "Crowns of Laurel" referred to in "The Satrapy"—the reward, perhaps, for his patience in not taking the road toward those illusive "things elsewhere."

We find further evidence to support the idea of an accommodation on Cavafy's part, of a new sense of the possibilities offered by Alexandria, in several poems that the poet first published in 1911, which proved to be an especially fruitful year for him. Eight poems entered the canon at that time, including "The God Abandons Antony," "The Glory of the Ptolemies," "Ithaka," "Ionic," and "The Ides of March." The first two of these are much to the point here. As I have already suggested, "The God

Abandons Antony" projects a godlike image of Alexandria, which replaces Dionysus and Hercules as the presiding deity of Antony's late world, the greatest gift he was given to know and his greatest loss at the hour of final defeat. A related, if hyperbolic, image of the city emerges from "The Glory of the Ptolemies":

I'm Lagides, king—through my power and wealth
complete master of the art of pleasure.
There's no Macedonian, no barbarian, equal to me
or even approaching me. The son of Selefkos
is really a joke with his cheap lechery.
But if you're looking for other things, note this too:
my city's the greatest preceptor, queen of the Greek world,
genius of all knowledge, of every art.

The Alexandria of these poems is not that small corner of the world that still tormented the poet in his 1907 note; it is, as the title here puts it, the city that was once the glory of the Ptolemies. But the fact that in 1911 Cavafy's mind turned not to London or any other contemporary city of hope but to the bright past of the city below his balcony window surely speaks in some measure for the accommodation he had reached since 1907. This return to the glories of the Alexandrian past (which I will explore more fully in chapter 4) appears to emerge at this time as an essential product of the new understanding, the new vision, that allowed the poet to transform a personal obsession with the confining and restricting aspects of his city first into a useful metaphor, then into a unique erotic landscape, and finally into a liberating myth—so liberating that by 1917 we find Cavafy publishing a poem that evokes his contemporary Alexandria in the kind of fond language the poet of a decade earlier could hardly have voiced without some irony:

Then, sad, I went out on to the balcony,
went out to change my thoughts at least by seeing
something of this city I love,
a little movement in the streets, in the shops.[15]

And it was in this year, 1917, that the poet chose to begin his thematic selections with "The City" and "The Satrapy."

Although the accommodation I have been outlining was first signalled by the transformation of Alexandria from subjective causal agent into more objective metaphor in the 1910 version of "The City," the aesthetic purgation that made this transformation possible had been a prolonged one, in process even before the 1894 draft of the poem. A review of Cavafy's development in this regard gives us a particular insight into his poetics, because what emerged from the process was both the personal voice and the major preoccupation of his mature poetry, the voice and the preoccupation that dominated his work after 1910. The first stage of the process was the gradual rejection of the simplistic Romantic imagery and imitative themes that abounded in the verse he wrote between 1884 and 1894, poems so ordinary that, as Seferis has suggested, it is difficult to see how this early work could in any way anticipate the poems offered by the mature Cavafy, who himself described much that he had written between the ages of nineteen and twenty-eight as "trash."[16] The titles of some of these early poems are almost enough by themselves to indicate the poet's derivative Romanticism: "Elegy of the Flowers" (1884), "Hours of Melancholy" (1892), "Voice from the Sea" (1893), "Good and Bad Weather" (1893), "In the House of the Soul" (1894), and "To the Moon" (1895—an acknowledged adaptation from Shelley).[17] One is tempted to follow Seferis's tongue-in-cheek counsel regarding these early poems and avoid offering translated excerpts from them, on the grounds that any translation, however inadequate, is likely to distort the original by improving it. But perhaps stanzas from two of the poems will give a sense of their limitations:

The loveliest flowers bloom in summer.
And of all the flowers of the field
youth shows as the most beautiful. But it withers quickly
and once it goes it does not come again;
the jasmine sprinkles it with the tears of dew.
    [First stanza of "Elegy of the Flowers"]

I hear sighs in the west winds.
I see complaints on the violets.
I feel the painful life of the rose,
the meadows filled with mysterious sorrow,
and in the dense woods a sob echoes.
    [Second stanza of "Hours of Melancholy"]

The primary source of the sentiments expressed in both these excerpts is probably Shelley: "The flower that smiles today / Tomorrow dies; / All that we wish to stay / Tempts and then flies," from "Mutability," and "Rough wind, that moanest loud / Grief too sad for song," from "A Dirge." But the sentiments had become so conventional and time-worn by Cavafy's day, as had the pathetic fallacy he chooses to exploit here, that it is perhaps not fair to place the full burden of influence on Shelley's shoulders. Nor is it likely that Shelley, even in his less inspired moments, would have allowed a metaphor as one-dimensional as "And of all the flowers of the field / youth shows as the most beautiful," or a line as precious as "the jasmine sprinkles it with the tears of dew," or a phrase as banal as "mysterious sorrow." In any case, since the poet did not allow any of the poems listed above to become part of the canon, they are of little interest to us now except as examples of what he had to purge, even as late as 1894, before he could begin to find the proper avenue for his talent. And a second dead end, that of late nineteenth-century aestheticism, though appearing a bit later in Cavafy's work, was bypassed after a few unacknowledged borrowings from Oscar Wilde, such as "Artificial Flowers" (1903):

I love flowers fashioned of glass or gold,
the faithful gifts of a faithful Art;
painted with colors more beautiful than those of nature,
wrought with mother-of-pearl and enamel,
the leaves and stems ideal.
Their grace comes from wise and purest Aestheticism . . .

More to the point for our purposes here is an early poem that did eventually win a place in the canon, "Candles" (1893), which, though primitive in its own way, does reveal the poet's attempt to move beyond simple nature imagery into a metaphoric landscape that is more alive and subtle:

Days to come stand in front of us
like a row of burning candles—
golden, warm, and vivid candles.

Days past fall behind us, a gloomy line of burnt-out candles;
the nearest are still smoking,
cold, melted, and bent.

I don't want to look at them: their shape saddens me,
and it saddens me to remember their original light.
I look ahead at my burning candles.

I don't want to turn, don't want to see, terrified,
how quickly that dark line gets longer,
how quickly one more dead candle joins another.

The central image here is obviously uncomplicated: the persona's future days are compared to a row of lighted candles and
his past days to a row of burned-out candles, the latter a sight
that he finds too terrifying to confront. The simile calls, perhaps,
for more suspension of disbelief than the sentiment it serves to
evoke really merits, but at least it is less conventional than the
nature imagery of other early poems quoted above, and the poet
develops his figure with just enough art and drama to hold our
interest.

A note that the poet wrote (in English) to his brother John at
about the time "Candles" was first published, in 1899, indicates
that Cavafy thought it "a good poem" and among those most
easily translatable into English, but the same note reveals a
rather self-conscious concern to have the mode of the poem
clearly understood so that its improbabilities will be accepted as
a legitimate exercise of literary license.[18] The note is important
for our purposes because it offers evidence of the poet's attempt,
not only in this poem but in others of the same period, to find a
form of expression that could translate personal "ennui" and
"desperance" into a more vital poetic imagery than his imitative
Romanticism and aestheticism permitted. After identifying the
mode of "Candles" as "visioniste" rather than "allegorical," he
explains to his brother in rather pedantic detail why the two
rows of candles cannot plausibly represent literal objects lighted
indefinitely in series, or partially burned out in series, but must be
taken as "a fleeting image on the mind" that is described "as it
comes" and that is not subject to "logical development" nor to
"all the limits of probability," because it does not make use of
"objects in action but objects in the form of images." He indicates that it is the "allegorical" mode of poems such as "Walls"
and "The Windows" that calls for a relatively strict fidelity to the
truth of objects and to the logical, plausible suggestion of the

primary meaning these objects are intended to convey ("confined life" in the case of both "Walls" and "The Windows").[19] The focus in an "allegorical" poem is on the object depicted, and since the poetic meaning of the object—the second term of the analogy—is not revealed overtly but only implied, the poet must use the object "logically, and with a fidelity to the primary meaning of its inanimate essence." The poem "Candles" is a different case, because the meaning is conveyed by overt comparison, and the second term of the comparison is offered explicitly:

In the poem under consideration, we are not writing about candles but about days. If we had gone against logic in something directly related to days, we would be worthy of the pit. But the candles are our image: the same correctness or exactness is not demanded of an image. We are not saying something impossible, because the existence of a row of lighted candles and a row of unlit candles is a thing entirely possible. We say that days are "like" those rows. That word "like" shows immediately that the candles are a simile, not an allegory.

The note tends to make the poem more elaborate than it actually is, and there is a defensiveness about it—especially on the question of plausibility—that seems to anticipate the later reevaluation of the poem, which resulted in its being excluded (unlike "The City," originally written only a year later) from his post-1911 collections. His development during the 1890s, in any case, followed the path of the "allegorical," rather than "visioniste," mode—an "allegorical" mode that is characterized by a focus on "objects in action" and by unstated analogies, and that the poet's letter to Pericles Anastasiadis defines as "suggestif." In the year after "Candles" was written, Cavafy wrote the first draft of "The City," two years later "Walls," and three years later "The Windows."[20] All three offer suggested analogies rather than overt comparisions. And all three offer an image of "confined life" through "objects in action," with the objects progressing from poem to poem toward more and more diminished space: from the streets, neighborhood, and house of "The City" to the huge high walls and the windowless rooms of the two later poems. It is not a very satisfactory progress. The analogy in "Walls" is so uncomplicated and two-dimensional that it provides sparse nourishment for the imagination. And the agents of speaker's predicament—an unspecified "they" posing as builders—are so ill-defined that his complaint sounds rather paranoid:

With no consideration, no pity, no shame,
they've built walls around me, thick and high.
And now I sit here feeling hopeless.
I can't think of anything else: this fate gnaws my mind—
because I had so much to do outside.
When they were building the walls, how could I not have noticed!
But I never heard the builders, not a sound.
Imperceptibly they've closed me off from the outside world.

The one subtle effect in the poem is the movement from a literal "object in action"—builders constructing walls around the poem's "I"—to the suggestive metaphoric extension of this "object" in the concluding lines: the sense that those mysterious forces at work, unheard and imperceptible, are not only imaginary but perhaps self-generated, a product of the "I's" own tormented psyche. By the end of the poem, it seems that he himself has become the unspecified "they" that oppress him, the mason of his own confinement. But the small mystery of this movement, in what remains a rather oversimplified and unmotivated context, is not enough to generate strong empathy or aesthetic excitement.

In the poem "The Windows," the "object in action" is even less complicated: a house without windows. And the analogous meaning, the "confined life," has even less subtlety and mystery because it is expressed overtly by the speaker:

In these dark rooms where I live out empty days,
I wander round and round
trying to find the windows.
It will be a great relief when a window opens.
But the windows aren't there to be found—
or at least I can't find them. And perhaps
it's better if I don't find them.
Perhaps the light will prove another tyranny.
Who knows what new things it will expose?

Again, the speaker's predicament, and his statement of it, leave little room for the reader's imagination: "I live out empty days" and "But the windows aren't there to be found—/ or at least I can't find them." The only metaphoric extension here, the only movement of interest, is toward the afterthought of the concluding lines, with their hint of an ultimate despair: a dark room without windows may be preferable to the new tyranny that light might bring.

The progress in the "allegorical" or "suggestif" poems—a progress at least by comparison to the imitative modes of Cavafy's earlier Romantic verse—apparently brought the poet to a dead end in 1897. The context of his objects in action had become smaller and smaller, not only offering less possibility for metaphoric or symbolic development but also an increasingly limited frame of reference outside the persona's psyche (in the first draft of "The City" there were at least those "people here" for him to hate, and in "Walls" a pitiless "they"). If "ennui" and "desperance" were to become the source for something more vital than the expression of an essentially subjective mood—what came to seem a rather paranoid complaint when restricted to the perspective of an "I" confined to a small, self-made prison—Cavafy had to find a mode more subtle and dramatic, and a frame of reference with broader social and symbolic possibilities, than these simple "allegories" permitted. We have already seen that by 1910 he was thoroughly aware of the need for depersonalizing the more subjective terms of the mood depicted in the first draft of "The City" and of the need for giving these terms a broader symbolic meaning. We have also seen evidence of the new route he chose to follow, in the 1905 poem "The Satrapy." But the breakthrough had actually come less than two years after he had written "The Windows," that is, in December 1898, with "Waiting for the Barbarians."

What seems most striking about this poem by comparison with earlier efforts is its dramatic mode, apparent from the first lines:

What are we waiting for, assembled in the forum?
  The barbarians are due here today.

The poet is not speaking here through a first-person mask or persona. What he gives us is a dramatic dialogue between two characters—the man in the street and his neighbor, if you will—observing a moment of history that neither can understand totally, though one is clearly more in the know than the other, and the poet makes use of the latter's knowledge to lead us in stages through the moment's drama. The rendering is entirely objective: the scene and its meaning are revealed without comment through the questions and answers of these two spectators. As their dialogue progresses, it becomes apparent that the poet does not have a specific city or a specific historical event in mind; his purpose is to offer an insight into the larger pattern of history that raises particular places and events to the level of metaphor or myth. The specific historical context is left deliberately vague; the only clues are the words "agora" and "barbarians," gradually reinforced by "senators," "emperor," "consuls," "praetors," and "orators," all of which suggest a Roman or early Byzantine context, but without precise geography or date. It becomes clear that our emperor and his retinue of officials, as well as his subjects gathered in the forum, are all citizens of an imaginary city, which is characterized by terms offered within the poem itself rather than by historical allusion. The senate in this city, once apparently active in making laws, seems more than willing to give up legislating even before it is forced to by the arriving barbarians. The emperor—up so early and now sitting in state at the main entrance to the city—also appears unusually eager to receive the expected barbarian leader and to flatter him with titles and imposing names. In fact, the city's style has been lately revised to accommodate what is assumed to be the barbarian taste: heavy on dazzling jewelry, light on rhetoric and public speaking. Along with the naive questioner in the poem, we cannot be certain why the emperor and his officials are so willing to accommodate the barbarians until the epigrammatic conclusion, "Those people were a kind of solution"—though there are tantalizing clues in the bewilderment and confusion that take over the citizenry when word arrives that there are no longer any barbarians. And the poet's method of dramatizing his theme projects an irony that lingers beyond the epigram: if life in this imaginary city has reached such a level of despair and futility and overrefinement that the advent of barbarians has become an eagerly awaited solution for both rulers and ruled, what hope can possibly be left for the powerless citizen when even this solution fails to materialize?

The new mode of this poem permitted Cavafy to make his point without having to intrude didactically or through a persona. The effect achieved is both more subtle and more suggestive than that which we saw in the "suggestif" renderings of his earlier mode. And the despair of earlier poems has been raised from a subjective to a communal context. Those small dramas of a confined psyche, rendered through objects in action, have been transformed into the larger drama of civilization in crisis rendered through characters, images, and symbols in action at a particular, significant moment in time. The terms of the crisis are revealed entirely through the drama depicted. On the one hand, the rulers of this satiated, overrefined civilization show, through action and gesture, that they are eager for any kind of change—even one that would allow their political power and their public style to be destroyed by barbarians about whom little is known other than that they are dazzled by jewelry and bored by rhetoric. On the other hand, the ruled of the same civilization show, again through action and gesture, that they are not only ready to accept the change their rulers are courting but are bewildered and apprehensive when the change does not take place. The last line is the only vaguely didactic touch, but it is spoken by a character participating in the action, and it depends, in any case, on symbolic values that have been subtly built into the term "barbarians" through the course of the poem.

The method developed in this poem provides for an exciting surface interest—a drama that holds the imagination—as well as a more general significance. And the experiment proved crucial: the poet's impulse toward objectivity and dramatic rendering, initiated in this poem, grew in strength during the decade that followed, and though the various modes that Cavafy chose to explore in responding to the impulse rarely produced poems as successful as "Waiting for the Barbarians," by the end of the decade he had perfected those modes that were to dominate his work throughout his mature years, specifically narrations, dramatic monologues, and first-person monologues in which the focus is not so much on a persona as on some object of the poet's discourse. All three of these modes facilitated his progress from subjectivity to objectivity; and all three were employed to make history, or fictionalized history, serve a metaphoric function. The narrations—poems in which the poet's voice is primarily that of a narrator recording an episode or outlining a character—were, during this period, either anecdotes about historical characters whose actions or gestures at a telling moment provide insight into their particular significance (for example, "Herodis Attikos," 1900, "King Dimitrios," 1900, "Manuel Komninos," 1905, and the "The Displeasure of Selefkidis," 1910) or brief biographies of historical characters whose careers illustrate some truth about the nature of politics or the historical process (for example, "Oropherns," 1904, and "Dimaratos," 1904). The several dramatic monologues of this period—a form of objective rendering influenced by Cavafy's reading in Browning and the Greek anthology—also make use of historical characters (usually minor figures on the peripheries of history) who not only reflect the taste and ethics of their times but become metaphors for perennial attitudes.[21] Cavafy's "Philhellene" (1906) is an apt case in point, one reminiscent of Browning both in its formal elements and in its representation of a historical context:

Make sure the engraving is done skillfully.
The expression serious, majestic.
The diadem preferably somewhat narrow:
I don't like that broad kind the Parthians wear.
The inscription, as usual, in Greek:
nothing excessive or pompous—
I don't want the proconsul to take it the wrong way;
he's always smelling things out and reporting back to Rome—
but of course giving me due honor.
Something very special on the other side:
maybe a discus-thrower, young, good-looking.
Above all I urge you to see to it
(Sithaspis, for God's sake don't let them forget)
that after "King" and "Savior,"
they add "Philhellene" in elegant characters.
Now don't try to be clever
with your "where are the Greeks?" and "what Hellenism
here behind Zagros, out beyond Phraata?"
Since so many others more barbarian than ourselves

Cavafy's Alexandria

choose to inscribe it, we'll inscribe it too.
And besides, don't forget that sometimes
sophists do come to us from Syria,
and versifiers, and other triflers of that kind.
So we're not, I think, un-Hellenized.

Technically the poem is very much in the Browning manner: a
self-revelation by the speaker in a particularized situation that
includes a listener addressed in the poem, with the poet's presence felt only through the mild irony that governs the speaker's
monologue. It could well be entitled "The King Orders his Coinage in the Land of Near-barbarians" to parallel Browning's "The
Bishop Orders his Tomb at Saint Praxed's Church." The self-
revealed character of the speaker ("nothing excessive or pompous . . . / but of course giving me due honor") creates only the
first level of interest; his call for elegant Greek characters and a
"young, good-looking" discus-thrower to adorn his coinage
serves, on another level, to define the taste of his times, much as
Browning's bishop defines the taste of his times by calling for
"Choice Latin, picked phrase, Tully's every word" and for "one
Pan / Ready to twitch the Nymph's last garment off" to adorn
his tomb. And if we cannot say that we learn as much about the
peripheral Hellenistic world east of Rome from Cavafy's short
monologue as Ruskin suggests we learn about the Italian Renais-
sance from Browning's considerably more elaborate monologue,
we nevertheless get a clear image of the historical context in
which Cavafy's speaker lives: a context in which, according to
Edwyn Bevan, the eastern rulers (specifically the Arsacids) "were
fain to present themselves to their Greek subjects as sympathetic
protectors" by stamping their coinage exclusively with Greek
legends, even if they were ultimately "unable to make the Greeks
overlook the difference between a barbarian and a western dynasty."[22] The petty monarch of this poem does not even have
Greek subjects to court, and that is in part the poem's point. Our
king's philhellenism is not so much political strategy as cultural
affectation and imitation ("Since so many others more barbarian
than ourselves / choose to describe it . . ."), akin to that of the
silent "Prince from Western Libya" and the other pseudo-phil-
hellenes in Cavafy's work, barbarian aristocrats whose small-

time snobbery—coupled with both a fear of, and an unlettered aspiration toward, the culture of Greece—merely dramatizes the distance a barbarian pretender has to travel in order to arrive at "the best of all things," as a true Hellene in a later poem describes the quality called Hellenic. The term "philhellene" becomes, in the context of this poem, a metaphor for the affectation of pretentious barbarian societies, just as the term "barbarians" became, in the earlier poem, a metaphor for the solutions desperately craved by advanced societies in decline.

As the juxtaposition of these two poems suggests, Cavafy had the capacity, from the beginning of his career as a "historical poet," to see the full spectrum of the historical process—and to see it objectively enough to discover the poetic metaphors in its vicissitudes.[23] What took him some time to discover (over a decade) was a structure that would make his metaphors, and the insights that went with them, more than a random series of poetic statements, more than a casual treasure hunt through the range of history that interested him. In the years immediately following "Waiting for the Barbarians," we find poems that make use of preclassical Greece ("The Funeral of Sarpedon," 1898; "When the Watchman Saw the Light," 1900; "Trojans," 1900; "Interruption," 1900; and "Unfaithfulness," 1903), Hellenistic Selefkia ("One of Their Gods," 1899), Athens in the second century A.D. ("Herodis Attikos," 1900), Thessaly-Locris in the fifth century B.C. ("Thermopylae," 1901), Constantinople in the fifteenth century A.D. ("Theophilos Palaiologos," 1903), the Peloponnese in Hellenistic times ("The Retinue of Dionysus," 1903), Syria in the second century B.C. ("Craftsman of Wine Bowls," 1903), Cappadocia in the second century B.C. ("Orophernis," 1904), Persia in the fifth century B.C. ("Dimaratos," 1904), Constantinople in the twelfth century A.D. ("Manuel Komninos," 1905), and on to the Persia of King Artaxerxes, the Italy of the Poseidonians, and the Rome of Julius Caesar. Time and place are very much in flux here; the poet is clearly shopping around for appropriate material in these years, picking out whatever strikes his fancy. In the end, the period that dominates this catalogue, the preclassical period, was the one that proved of least interest to the poet in his maturity, as did settings in mainland Greece. And he delayed further exploitation of Byzantine sources for some twelve years after "Manuel Komninos." There is really no way of predicting, from the varied time and place of these poems, that Cavafy would choose to focus, during the second decade of the century, almost exclusively on Hellenistic Greece, with the city of Alexandria as his focal point. The clue to his choice, and to the structure that gave it shape, lies not so much in the historian's preference for certain dates and settings as in the poet's increasingly sophisticated approach to metaphor during the first decade of the century. In short, Cavafy's progress toward the specific time and place that dominate his poetry from 1910 on seems to follow naturally from his developing use of a communal context to provide the structure for his metaphoric statements: a progress from a confined persona to an imaginary metaphoric city, and from this city to others with a more defined historical—but still symbolic—identity, a progress culminating, at the end of the decade, in the crucial city of his poetic imagination, the city most capable of rising out of metaphor and into myth—Alexandria.

We have already seen the first stage of this progress in the transition from the small subjective world of "Walls," "The Windows," and the 1894 draft of "The City" to the imaginary city of "Waiting for the Barbarians," written in 1898.[24] A further stage is apparent in an "unpublished" poem written two years later, "When the Watchman Saw the Light." The context of this poem is more historically precise and familiar (also considerably less imaginative); it is the scene described by Aeschylus at the beginning of *Agamemnon*, when the watchman sees the light signalling the victory of the Greeks at Troy and the imminent return of Agamemnon to meet his death at the hands of his wife, Clytemnestra. Though an aspect of the poem's theme is reminiscent of "Waiting for the Barbarians"—no phase of civilization is eternal, including the dynasty of well-established, ancient houses such as the grand house of Atreus—there is a significant development here in the poet's use of a communal context: the one element of this civilization that seems likely to survive the changing fortunes of its rulers is the city of Argos. The house of Atreus is as doomed as any other, but "Argos can do without the house of Atreus" because Argos knows that new rulers just as indispensable, unique, and great as the old "can always be found at a moment's notice." In this poem the city is made a metaphor for the communal wisdom that comes with what some would call political cynicism and others a proper insight into the ways of the world as illuminated by the patterns of local history. The point, for our purposes, is that Cavafy focuses here for the first time on the metaphoric possibilities of an actual city, identified by name and by the particular historical background that defines it.

A second poem written in the same year, "Trojans" (1900), is a more complicated example of the same development. The historical context appears initially in a simile: "our efforts are like those of the Trojans," that is, those of men prone to disaster; and the context becomes more precise with the allusion to Achilles in the second stanza. But as the poem progresses, Cavafy's subtle manipulation of the parallel between contemporaneity and antiquity causes the poem's "we" and their historical counterparts to merge so completely that by the end of the poem the stated terms of the initial simile have disappeared. The poem's contemporary "we" come to live (and soon to die) within the environs of the ancient city that symbolizes their fate:

Our efforts are like those of the Trojans.
We think we'll change our luck
by being resolute and daring,
so we move outside ready to fight.

But when the big crisis comes,
our boldness and resolution vanish;
our spirit falters, paralyzed,
and we scurry around the walls
trying to save ourselves by running away.

Yet we're sure to fail. Up there,
high on the walls, the dirge has already begun.
They're mourning the memory, the aura of our days.
Priam and Hecuba mourn for us bitterly.

The image of the city is veiled here, yet its presence is crucial: the activity "up there, / high on the walls" again represents a continuity and wisdom that live beyond the particular disasters of the moment. The fate of the poem's "we" has already been absorbed and accommodated by the community inside the walls; even before these men, so prone to disaster, have encountered the inevitable death that lies in wait for them, "the dirge has already begun" and the city is in mourning for "the memory, the aura of [their] days." As Argos survives the demise of its indispensable leaders, so the Troy of this poem survives the fate of its doomed Trojans. And in both poems it is the metaphoric image of the city that provides both the dramatic context and the precise history for a potentially didactic—and therefore excessively subjective—statement about the human condition.

The several poems that complete the progress I have been outlining share the same form, one that gives us further evidence of Cavafy's effort during the first decade of the century to find ways of moving from the subjective to the dramatic while still maintaining a stance that would allow him to press home his point. These poems make use of a persona who addresses a character in the second person, offering advice and drawing conclusions in terms of the context the poem projects—what one might call a "didactic monologue" for short. The earliest example of this form is the second stanza of the 1894 draft of "The City," and the latest, two poems written in 1910, "Ithaka" and "The God Abandons Antony."[25] It is, therefore, a form only sparsely represented in the canon of post-1911 poems, one abandoned early in Cavafy's mature years in favor of narrations, dramatic monologues, and first-person monologues such as those that focus on contemporary Alexandria. But it is partly the poet's stance in these so-called "second person" poems that allows us to identify his point of view about the imagery that he was creating during this period; the poet's point of view becomes, in these poems, an overt aspect of the statements they make, though his attitude comes over palatably because it focuses always on the context dramatized.

We first heard this variation of the poet's voice in the second stanza of "The City," telling the poem's "I" that he will "always end up in this city" and should therefore give up hope for "things elsewhere." And we heard it again in "The Satrapy," telling the poem's "you" what the "you" already knows: that his heart is aching for things he will never find in his satrapy because they reside in the city he has too hastily abandoned. The poet's stance in both poems permits him to offer a commentary within the dramatic structure he has established, one that suggests the accommodation that Cavafy himself was able to make with his own city. And the two poems are the earliest to depict in detail a landscape of the symbolic territory that the city image represents during this period: the "black ruins" and inescapable neighborhoods of "The City," and "the Agora, the Theatre, the Crowns of Laurel" that the protagonist of "The Satrapy" has left behind him. But it is not until "Ithaka" (1910) that the poet's commentary within the poem actually assigns a symbolic value to the image that he has been developing for some years. The image in this poem is an extension of that represented in "The Satrapy." The poet's voice again addresses the poem's "you"—in this case a Ulysses figure—with advice regarding the road he is about to take, not to Susa but back home to Ithaka. This advice suggests another side of the attitude expressed in "The Satrapy": you may long for what you left behind in your home country, but in making your way back to those "Crowns of Laurel," be sure to take your time, be sure to get the most you can out of the long journey home, because the experience of that journey is what counts most and what finally defines the value of the city to which you are returning (an island-city in this case):

Keep Ithaka always in your mind.
Arriving there is what you're destined for.
But don't hurry the journey at all.
Better if it lasts for years,
so you're old by the time you reach the island,
wealthy with all you've gained on the way,
not expecting Ithaka to make you rich.

Ithaka gave you the marvelous journey.
Without her you wouldn't have set out.
She has nothing left to give you now.

And if you find her poor, Ithaka won't have fooled you.
Wise as you will have become, so full of experience,
You'll have understood by then what these Ithakas mean.

Again we see Cavafy turning the myths of history around to show us what may lie behind the façade most familiar to us. The long Odyssean voyage, full of monsters, frustrations, and long-ings for home in the Homeric tradition, becomes, in Cavafy's new world, "the marvelous journey," "full of adventure, full of discovery" and free of "Laistrygonians, Cyclops, / wild Posei-don" if only you can be made to realize its true possibilities by keeping "your thoughts raised high" and your spirit open to rare excitement. And the island-city at the end of the journey, tradi-tionally the home paradise whose memory torments the voyager and compels him to move on despite the obstacles and tempta-tions in his way, becomes the symbolic home of the voyager's destiny, a beginning more than an end: perhaps poor in itself, but of value as the impetus for the marvelous journey home. Ithaka's wealth is in the motive she provided—and that is what these home cities, "these Ithakas," really "mean" for those open to adventure and discovery. We seem here to have come full circle from the attitude of "The City," which provided no road out of the home city that the protagonist, confined to its neigh-borhoods, desperately hoped to escape; but in fact the two poems are opposite sides of the same coin. The metaphoric city is still what you make it in your soul: for those who can see around them only the black ruins of their lives, there is no escape from the small corner their psyches have created, while for those who keep their thoughts raised high and their spirit and body tuned for rare excitement, the city can become the impetus for a great voyage that will lead them through pleasure and knowl-edge to an understanding, among other things, of their city's metaphoric significance—in this case the reflection of their elevated, adventurous spirit.

The poet's use of the plural "Ithakas" in the concluding line of the poem emphasizes the generalized, symbolic character of the image he has projected in the poem: not just this island-city, home to Ulysses, but all places with the power to stir a voyager's imagination and fulfill his destiny. This is the most overt instance of such symbolic generalization offered by the poet's own voice within a poem. Cavafy wisely decided that one effec-tive use of this rhetorical device was all he could afford. His strategy from this point forward was to narrow in on a specific city and to build the image of that particular city from poem to poem, without generalized comment and almost entirely through narrations and dramatic monologues, until the metaphoric associations that gathered around the image began to shape a central myth. The city he chose was of course Alexandria, which at this time began to dominate the poet's consciousness on two planes at once, the ancient and the contemporary. The poem that establishes the ancient plane is "The God Abandons Antony," written one month after "Ithaka" in the same didactic monologue form, though the didactic element is handled in a way that effects one of the most subtle and moving statements in the Cavafy canon:

At midnight, when suddenly you hear
an invisible procession going by
with exquisite music, voices,
don't mourn your luck that's failing now,
work gone wrong, your plans
all proving deceptive—don't mourn them uselessly:
as one long prepared, and full of courage,
say goodbye to her, to Alexandria who is leaving.
Above all, don't fool yourself, don't say
it was a dream, your ears deceived you:
don't degrade yourself with empty hopes like these.
As one long prepared, and full of courage,
as is right for you who were given this kind of city,
go firmly to the window
and listen with deep emotion,
but not with the whining, the pleas of a coward;
listen—your final pleasure—to the voices,
to the exquisite music of the strange procession,
and say goodbye to her, to the Alexandria you are losing.

The poet's imperative voice, telling Antony how he is to behave in his last moments, is largely a mask for the evocation, the deification, of the city that is at the heart of the poem. The deification begins with Cavafy's transformation of the historical sources that give the poem its plot: his substitution of the god Alexandria for Dionysus and Hercules as the presiding deity of Antony's last days.[26] Alexandria is the god that the great Roman had come to worship, or more precisely, the god he had proven himself worthy of worshiping once the gift of the city was given him (these are the several implications of the Greek ποὺ ἀξιώϑη-κες μιὰ τέτοια πόλι). And it is this god who now abandons him in his defeat through the appropriate means of a "final pleasure": the exquisite music of an invisible procession. For the phrase "final pleasure" implies all the earlier pleasures that have come to define "this kind of city" and that must now go the way of all the divine things on earth that mortals are doomed to lose in their hour of ultimate defeat. But what also defines this kind of city and those worthy of knowing it is the ability to see things for what they are, honestly and courageously, even when what one sees is the inevitable loss of all else that the city has come to represent. The only thing "right for you who were given this kind of city" is to face the reality beyond the window without self-deception and without hope, but with the courage to feel deeply the last exquisite manifestation of the divine life you are losing.

Many of the essential terms of Cavafy's Alexandrian myth are implicit in this last didactic monologue, the culmination of the poet's early progress toward a vital and original metaphoric structure. The decade that followed the writing of this poem was devoted in large part to the elaboration, extension, and further dramatization of its implications, within the context of both the contemporary city below Cavafy's balcony window and the ancient city that gave focus to his unique survey of Greek history.

chapter three

The Sensual City

In reviewing the many poems by Cavafy that make use of the poet's contemporary Alexandria, one encounters certain curious circumstances that provide insight into the general intention and pattern of the poet's continuing "work in progress" (to quote Seferis again) during his mature years. To begin with, the poems set in contemporary Alexandria, unlike many of the poems that treat this city and others historically, focus on erotic themes to the exclusion of all others.[1] But the focus remains hesitant and partial in some respects. Though Cavafy began writing personal love poetry as early as 1904, he did not start to publish contemporary erotic poems until 1912, and a number of the more seemingly subjective poems of this kind (for example, those in which a first-person voice addresses or comments on a specific lover or potential lover) never appeared in print during his lifetime. And once he began to publish erotic poems situated in the city outside his window, he did so consistently throughout his career, revising and printing poems originally written in previous years (as much as ten years earlier in some instances) along with current work, so as to offer some erotic poems set in contemporary Alexandria under each of his annual groupings in the folders he distributed to his select audience of readers.[2]

This history suggests several things about Cavafy's development. First of all, his erotic vision and his view of the city outside his window had merged almost totally by the time he came to publish erotic poems set in the contemporary city, so that modern Alexandria, at least as depicted in his work, had become for him an image of the Sensual City. Secondly, he began to write more or less personal love poetry earlier than has been assumed by those who have had only the chronology of his publications for a guide, but he deliberately delayed revealing the particular context of his eroticism for some years—until he was roughly fifty—and the pattern of revelation, once he decided to make it a pattern, was carefully controlled so that it progressed in stages from the general and implicit to the more specific and overt, though never far enough to include poems in which a first-person speaker was an active participant in a context that established the sex of the loved one unambiguously.[3] And once Cavafy decided to reveal the dimensions of his Sensual City

(1912-13 being the beginning of his substantial commitment in this direction), he apparently planned his work so that his readers would have before them a more-or-less continuous image of contemporary Alexandria alongside the historical and mythic territory his city served to evoke. In this way they could not help keeping one eye directed at the poet's version of the actual city outside his window while they were being transported, through adjacent poems, into the world of history and myth beyond.

These circumstances seem to indicate two impulses at work. In 1904 Cavafy evidently made a crucial decision to break through some of the "obstacles" (as he called them in "Hidden Things," 1908)[4] that were preventing him from writing what he really wanted to write about the life of his contemporary city—a decision to express his particular eroticism more openly and personally, at least in work for his own eyes. The second decision, some eight years later, to begin publishing more or less candid erotic poems, and to do so with increasing—if never total—candor, would seem to indicate a further extension of this impulse, an attempt to begin to "act freely" as an artist (to quote from the same poem), however imperfect and bigoted he might find the society in which he lived. But what is more important, by 1912-13 Cavafy had discovered a method for making the revelation of his eroticism something more than simply a question of confession and self-justification (as the Alexandrian critic Timos Malanos misleadingly views his revelation)[5]—a method that allowed him, after 1911, to bring the contemporary Sensual City into the mainstream of his verse.[6]

It was this impulse—to withhold his revelation until it could serve a broader artistic purpose and then to control the subjective, confessional aspect of the revelation once the purpose was in progress—that emerged as the significant impulse behind his poetic use of anomalous eroticism. The broader artistic purpose I have in mind is the unique version of the "mythical method" that Cavafy offers us after 1912, a version related to, but rather different from, the method that Yeats, Joyce, Pound, and Eliot had begun to practice at much the same time. Eliot defined the "mythical method" as the manipulation of "a continuous parallel between contemporaneity and antiquity" through what Joyce called "two-plane" writing.[7] But instead of carrying the parallel

Cavafy's Alexandria

forward in simultaneous, superimposed images, as his Irish and American contemporaries did (Ulysses-Bloom confronting Nausicaa-Gerty MacDowell, or Elpenor-Mauberley with his epitaph on an oar, or Stetson in the ships at Mylae), Cavafy juxtaposes an ancient city and a contemporary city in parallel poems, published and distributed more or less simultaneously, the pairing a continuous process, with the image of one city paralleling the other year after year. This suggests that the revelation of the poet's Sensual City was carefully plotted for more than merely personal reasons, however compelling Cavafy's need to reveal "hidden things" may have become between 1904 and 1912. It also suggests that the reader of Cavafy's poems is not reading him in full depth unless he is aware that the poems were arranged so as to offer a "two-plane" image of Alexandria. My discussion will necessarily focus on the two planes independently, beginning with the contemporary city that Cavafy began to create in 1904; but this image and that of his historical-mythical cities actually functioned together after 1911 to establish the vision that characterizes the poet's mature work.

The erotic poems that Cavafy began writing in 1904 strike us as uniquely candid in context and attitude, not only by comparison to conventional love poetry in English at the turn of the century, but by comparison to what Cavafy himself thought might pass for love poetry when he first started writing—for example, these rather droll stanzas from "When, my Friends, I was in Love" (1885), gallantly heterosexual and hyperbolic in keeping with the folk tradition the young poet was attempting to honor, even if he chose to do so in a hybrid mixture of purist (*katharevousa*) and demotic Greek:*

---

*Cavafy stopped writing poems in purist Greek early in his career, though puristic elements remained even in his mature work. The Greek of the poems discussed in this study is quite special, with a personal flavor that varies from poem to poem and that inevitably escapes both translation and effective description. In the most general terms, one can say that Cavafy's Greek is a slightly formalized demotic, with puristic coloring at moments in both inflections and choice of words, with occasional syntactical echoes of the poet's Constantinopolitan background and of Alexandrian usage, and with certain personal eccentricities here and there in word order and construction. One also finds colloquialisms, usually introduced into a more formal context in order to create a particular rhetorical effect, for example, to underline a satirical tone. In short, though Cavafy's Greek at times ap-

The dress she wore
was of cheap calico
yet to me I swear it seemed
fashioned of sheer silk.

Two common bracelets
adorned her arms;
I saw them as ornaments
for the noble and wealthy.

Flowers from the mountain
wreathed her head;
what bouquet could offer
such adornment to me?

The genius of orators and wise men
cannot persuade me now
as one gesture of hers could
in those days gone by.

Admittedly this is no more than a curious exercise written by
the poet when he was twenty-two years old—and mercifully it
bore no offspring. He quickly abandoned the exploitation of
"conventional" love, except for that of the "beautiful Circassian
girl" of "Blue Eyes" (1892), that of the Athenian courtesan dazzled by her eloquent Italian lover in "Horace in Athens" (1893),
and that of the lovers in his adaptation of Lady Anne Barnard's
ballad "Auld Robin Grey" entitled "A Love" (1896). Less conventional, perhaps, are the passion of Salome in the poem of
that name written in 1896, the "terrible and beautiful passion" of "Bouquets" (1897), and the "sensual fever" of "Chande-
lier" (1895), the latter an interesting poem because it offers a
very early (if impersonal) reference to the "passionate longing"
that has its source in lust that "isn't for timid bodies"—though
the poet didn't allow this first celebration of daring lust to appear in print until nineteen years after it was written, that is,
until the true context of his eroticism had already begun to manifest itself in other published poems.

---

pears more formal and idiosyncratic than the prevalent demotic of his contemporary poets on the mainland, and though it reveals a certain influence
from his diaspora background and his lifelong residence in Alexandria, he
made subtle use of the particular language he inherited for tonal effects, and
he was among the first of Greek poets in this century to recognize the poetic
values of a colloquial idiom.

Except for these instances, Eros cannot be called a significant theme in Cavafy's work until the several "unpublished" poems of 1904.[8] Three of these, "September, 1903," "December, 1903," and "January, 1904"—probably inspired by the poet's memories of a visit to Athens in 1903—are personal love lyrics without a precise evocation of place or a distinct narrative line.[9] But two others, "On the Stairs" and "At the Theatre," establish the context and the voice that will be exploited in one form or another throughout the poet's mature work, even if the use of the second person allows an ambiguity regarding the sex of the figure addressed. The first, "On the Stairs", introduces us to the quarter of Alexandria that one might call the grubby heart of Cavafy's Sensual City:

As I was going down those ill-famed stairs
you were coming in the door, and for a second
I saw your unfamiliar face and you saw mine.
Then I hid so you wouldn't see me again,
and you hurried past me, hiding your face,
and slipped inside the ill-famed house
where you couldn't have found pleasure any more than I did.

And yet the love you were looking for, I had to give you;
the love I was looking for—so your tired, knowing eyes
    implied—
you had to give me.
Our bodies sensed and sought each other;
our blood and skin understood.

But we both hid ourselves, flustered.

The setting will become characteristic as Cavafy builds his image of the Sensual City: that quarter the poet describes, perhaps a bit elaborately, as "the quarter that lives / only at night, with orgies and debauchery, / with every kind of intoxication and desire," when the city becomes transformed into the Hellenistic Selefkia of "One of Their Gods." The literal setting he has in mind is very likely that of the Quartier Attarine, which the poet came to know intimately in his early years, its narrow side streets lined with brothels that could accommodate all variety of sexual need, except, maybe, the flash of desire between two reticent strangers meeting by chance, as in the poem just quoted. Sexual encounters between strangers, one of the repeated dramas in Cavafy's contemporary city, normally take place in surroundings that seem less obvious or propitious: in a crowd near a lighted tobacco-shop window (as in "The Window of the Tobacco Shop," 1907), or in a corner of a taverna (as in "Comes to Rest," 1918), or in a small shop offering cheap merchandise for workers (as in "He Asked about the Quality," 1930). Brothels are perhaps less hospitable to the evocation of that particular excitement that comes with the sudden recognition of mutual desire between strangers and the quick response to it, sometimes made the more compelling when the desire must have its way despite the presence of a latent danger:

It must have been one o'clock at night
or half past one.
                    A corner in a taverna,
behind the wooden partition:
except for the two of us the place completely empty.
A lamp barely gave it light.
The waiter was sleeping by the door.

No one could see us.
But anyway, we were already so worked up
we'd become incapable of caution.

Our clothes half opened—we weren't wearing much:
it was a beautiful hot July.

Delight of flesh between
half-opened clothes;
quick baring of flesh—a vision
that has crossed twenty-six years
and now comes to rest in this poetry.
                    ["Comes to Rest," 1918]

The same sense of heightened desire in unpropitious surroundings comes through in the late poem "He Asked About the Quality" (1930), where the action is depicted as furtive and secretive because of a latent danger, but where the poet's evocation of it seems to gain intensity from just that circumstance:

He asked about the quality of the handkerchiefs
and how much they cost, his voice choking,
almost silenced by desire.
And the answers came back in the same mood,
distracted, the voice hushed,
offering hidden consent.

Cavafy's Alexandria

They kept on talking about the merchandise—
but the only purpose: that their hands might touch
over the handkerchiefs, that their faces, their lips,
might move close together as though by chance—
a moment's meeting of limb against limb.

Quickly, secretly, so the shopowner sitting at the back
wouldn't realize what was going on.

But the sexual encounters in Cavafy's contemporary city are
not always between strangers, nor is the realized desire of lovers
confined to furtive release in hidden places. The poem that best
dramatizes an unqualified pleasure, "Two Young Men, 23 to 24
Years Old" (1927), portrays lovers who have apparently shared
a "sensitive" love for some time, and it shows them leaving a
café, "all joy and vitality, feeling and charm," in order to spend
a long night giving themselves to drink and love in what the poet
calls "a familiar and very special / house of debauchery" where
they'd obviously known joy before. This house, and another
boasting "secret rooms / considered shameful even to name" in
"And I Lounged and Lay on Their Beds" (1915), were very likely
inspired by what Cavafy knew of the Quartier Attarine and the
bisexual brothels on its narrow side streets—streets that would
hardly seem to offer the possibility of joy and fulfilment, as the
poem "On the Stairs" suggests. Yet the poet's Sensual City has
many mansions, and some of those housing the fullest pleasures
are to be found in the more sordid neighborhoods. In fact, the
poet's images of the "ideal" or "perfect" in matters of love
(among his favorite and least satisfactory adjectives) are seen to
blossom forth most readily in rather mucky soil. It is partly a
question of contrasts—of the ideal set in relief by its proximity to
the vulgar—partly the reflection of a romantic (and not entirely
convincing) supposition that the sordid or the shabby contains a
particular beauty and vitality, even a secret purity, under the
veil of its visible surface. The characteristic citizen of Cavafy's
contemporary city—the figure "shaped for and dedicated to the
Hellenic kind of pleasure," as he puts it in "The Photograph"
(1913)—is a drifter leading "a degrading, vulgar life" in "horrible" surroundings, generally on the move from one shabby
setting to another, whether a low café, a cheap taverna, an ironmonger's shop, or a room in some "shameless" house. Yet it is in

these very "waste land" surroundings that the drifting figure seems most capable of revealing a "perfect" beauty (as in "Days of 1909, '10, and '11," 1928), the virginal remnant in his much used body (as in "Days of 1901," 1927), "the pure sensuality of his pure flesh" (as in "Days of 1896," 1925), or a kind of fulfilment that transcends time (as in "One Night," 1907):

The room was cheap and sordid,
hidden above the suspect taverna.
From the window you could see the alley,
dirty and narrow. From below
came the voices of workmen
playing cards, enjoying themselves.

And there on that ordinary, plain bed
I had love's body, knew those intoxicating lips,
red and sensual,
red lips so intoxicating
that now as I write, after so many years,
in my lonely house, I'm drunk with passion again.

The poet's "lonely house" in the year this poem was written had just become his second-story apartment with a balcony on the Rue Lepsius, which was crossed by narrow streets that offered a number of brothels somewhat more bourgeois and respectable (the whores mostly French) than those of the Quartier Attarine, but gamy enough to give the district a certain notoriety even in the great "winepress of love" (as Durrell called his Alexandria).[10] Those on intimate terms with Cavafy's poetry would find nothing inappropriate about his deciding to move into a neighborhood of that kind, nor would they regard convenience (his office, the Greek patriarchate and hospital, and several of his favorite cafés were not far) or reasonable rent the only motives for his remaining there even after the ground floor of his own building began to house whores bold enough to wave to him and his visitors as they approached the entrance. Cavafy is reported to have said about his ill-famed neighbors: "Poor things. One must be sorry for them. They receive some disgusting people, some monsters, but [and his voice took on a deep, ardent tone] they receive some angels, some angels!" It is also reported that he thought of moving elsewhere ("Shall I leave, or shall I put in electric light?"), but the fact is that he remained there for the last twenty-six years of his life, and one suspects that he did so because he found it his kind of territory. "Where could I live better," he once said. "Below, the brothel caters for the flesh. And there is the church which forgives sin. And there is the hospital where we die."[11]

There, also, are the streets that carry the imagination to the heart of the contemporary city that Cavafy recreated in his poetry, the city of memories, shaped almost entirely by sensual images out of the past, as the poet himself suggests in one of his more personal and revealing poems, "In the Evening" (1916), when a letter he is reading brings back echoes from his "days of indulgence" and the "wonderful life," the "magnificent bed," he'd shared with a young lover—echoes from the past that finally move him to find solace in the literal city below his second story window, as though to reassure himself that the images he has just celebrated are not merely the product of a fanciful nostalgia but belong to the history of a living reality made up of streets and shops that he can still actually see:

I picked up a letter again,
read it over and over till the light faded.
Then, sad, I went out on to the balcony,
went out to change my thoughts at least by seeing
something of this city I love,
a little movement in the streets, in the shops.

For the poet to have to *see*, at least, the literal city he loves in order to change his thoughts suggests how little he has been experiencing that city directly and how much his thoughts have been confined to the city of the imagination—that other city his memory has once again roused, the product of the mind's eye transforming the reality below the window into a personal poetic image, what we might call, for short, his city of remembered sensations. Cavafy implies in the late poem "In the Same Space" (1929) that the literal city is finally important only as a source for this other city, which became a thing the poet *created*, a thing that the play of his imagination through the years finally metamorphosed into pure feeling:

The setting of houses, cafés, the neighborhood
that I've seen and walked through years on end:

I created you while I was happy, while I was sad,
with so many incidents, so many details.

And, for me, the whole of you has been transformed into feeling.

What are the specific characteristics of this contemporary
Alexandria that the poet created? To begin with, his city of
remembered sensations draws as much on imagined as on actual
experience. The poet's imagination is not only an agent transforming what he sees below his balcony window into a poetic
image; it is also a principal actor in the series of dramas that
make up the life of the city he projects. As he tells us in "I
Went" (1905), the pleasures he goes to with such abandon in "the
brilliant night" of his Alexandria are pleasures "half real, / half
wrought by my own mind." And in the unpublished poem
"On Hearing of Love" (1911), his speaker admonishes an imaginary listener to remember, on hearing about great love, "how
much your imagination created for you": those less real and tan-
gible but even greater loves experienced by the mind's eye alone.
The interplay—sometimes the tension—between imagination
and actuality, or illusion and reality, is a major concern in the
sensual world that Cavafy created, and it is introduced at the
very beginning of his conception in "At the Theatre," the second
of the two unpublished Alexandrian poems that Cavafy wrote in
1904, the year his image of the contemporary city first began to
take shape. The setting here, though neither a brothel nor a
secret retreat, is equally appropriate to his image because it
serves as a kind of metaphor for the theatre of the mind, where
one half of his sensuality found its home during these years:

I got bored looking at the stage
and raised my eyes to the box circle.
In one of the boxes I saw you
with your strange beauty, your decadent youthfulness.
My thoughts turned back at once
to all I'd heard about you that afternoon;
my mind and body were aroused.
And as I gazed enthralled
at your languid beauty, your languid youthfulness,

your tastefully discriminating dress,
in my imagination I kept picturing you
the way they'd talked about you that afternoon.

As I have pointed out elsewhere, the theatrical performance that enthralls the speaker in this poem is not that which he sees on the actual stage before him but that which he sees on the stage of his own imagination, where his mind "pictures" the object of his attention the way they'd talked about him that afternoon—no doubt scandalously.[12] But it is also characteristic of Cavafy's mode to establish a sense of actual physical presence—of beauty felt and admired—before allowing the imagination to have its moment on stage. The progress is almost inevitably from observed physical details—albeit sometimes rather nonspecific—to the mind's ruminations, as though the imagination cannot perform its metamorphic function, its translation into aroused feeling, unless it has roots in a physical reality.

Another unpublished poem, "Half an Hour" (1917), offers an even more explicit, and more complex, dramatization of this theme:

I never had you, nor I suppose
will I ever have you. A few words, an approach,
as in the bar yesterday—nothing more.
It's sad, I admit. But we who serve Art,
sometimes with the mind's intensity
can create pleasure that seems almost physical—
but of course only for a short time.
That's how in the bar yesterday—
mercifully helped by alcohol—
I had half an hour that was totally erotic.
And I think you understood this
and stayed slightly longer on purpose.
That too was very necessary.
Because with all the imagination,
all the magic alcohol,
I needed to see your lips as well,
needed your body near me.

The setting of the poem, a bar, brings us back to familiar territory, as does the action: a brief encounter between strangers involving a few words, an approach. But in this case the approach does not lead to physical contact (as it does in other poems, for example "The Window of the Tobacco Shop," "Comes to Rest," and "He Asked about the Quality"), and that fact becomes the heart of the matter. The speaker admits he is sorry the encounter did not progress further than it did, yet the lines that follow this admission come very close to suggesting the contrary. When there is no contact, the imagination is free to move on stage without strong competition from an actual physical reality, and for those who serve Art, this allows the mind to create an erotic pleasure, which, if only *almost* physical, nevertheless proves to be "total" or "perfect" (the Greek permits either rendering). One wonders whether the speaker, for all his sadness, would make the same claim for any actual experience that left less to the imagination. He implies that the artist-lover, by intensity of mind, can know that which the lover pure and simple is unlikely to know, however realized and physically rewarding his erotic encounters. Perfect and total erotic experiences in Cavafy's city are reserved, it would seem, for those residents who keep at least one eye open to the world of the mind, the world of fantasy. At the same time, this poem reinforces an implication seen in the last: that however total or perfect an imagined erotic experience, that experience requires a sense of the loved one's physical presence to be complete: "I needed to see your lips as well, / needed your body near me."

As this poem and "At the Theatre" suggest, there is a constant division, in Cavafy's image of contemporary experience, between the satisfactions of fantasy and those of actuality. Ecstasy and perfection normally belong to the world of fantasy or the world of memory, while the actual life of his city, as it emerges in the narrative background to his heightened recollections, is usually partial and doomed, a waste land peopled by frustrations, ephemeral encounters, pleasures that are to a degree unfulfilled, or shabby, or, most important of all, transient. As Seferis has said, Cavafy's is a personal waste land without Eliot's forgotten myths and with only two symbols left, "the dead Adonis who is not restored to life—the sterile Adonis, and Proteus, old, exhausted and sick—the 'Fisher-King', who can no longer take on different shapes."[13] The memories are those of

Proteus, the actual experiences those of the unresurrected Adonis. Sterility, frustration, loss: these are the prevailing attributes of actual experience in Cavafy's contemporary city. Frustration is there from the very start, in 1904: "Our bodies sensed and sought each other; / our blood and skin understood. / But we both hid ourselves, flustered." And a few years later, in 1909, there is the inevitable pattern of loss—chance discovery, quick parting, painful and futile longing:

I never found them again—all lost so quickly . . .
the poetic eyes, the pale face . . .
in the darkening street . . .
I didn't find them any more—mine entirely by chance,
and so easily given up,
then longed for so painfully.
The poetic eyes, the pale face,
those lips—I didn't find them any more.
["Days of 1903"]

This pattern—the chance encounter followed by an affair that ends quickly and abruptly and is replaced by a painful longing that is ultimately transmuted into exquisite remembrance— becomes the dramatic focus of poem after poem. "In the Evening" (1916), the poem that brings the first-person speaker out on to his balcony to look at the city he loves, begins: "It wouldn't have lasted long anyway—/ years of experience make that clear. / But Fate did put an end to it a bit abruptly. / It was soon over, that wonderful life. / Yet . . . "—and the speaker goes on to depict its wonder, followed by an image of his sad, lingering act of recollection. The affair mentioned in "Gray" (1917) lasted a month, and the lovers never met again, but we are told that perhaps the poet's memory can bring back what was lost, unchanged despite the ravages of time. In "The Twenty-fifth Year of His Life" (1918), the protagonist is "sick with longing" for one of the "shady young types" he'd met only the previous month and has lost already. The protagonist of "In Despair" (1923), having lost his lover so completely that it seems "as though he never existed"—this because the lover wanted to save himself "from the tainted, sick form of sexual pleasure"—now tries desperately to recapture what he has lost vicariously, through fantasy, with each new lover who comes his way. The frustration and despair in "A Young Poet in his Twenty-fourth Year" (1928) are of a rather different kind: the two lovers are not "equally given to the abnormal form of pleasure," and as a consequence, the protagonist, who is the one "completely possessed by it," finds his brain consumed not by work but by the "one-sided passion" that is "destroying him." What frustrates the affair in "Lovely White Flowers" (1929) is death itself, though the bargaining that has gone on to keep the affair alive hardly inspires confidence that it would have lasted very long anyway. Finally, in "Before Time Altered Them" (1924), we see a dying affair salvaged, in a way, when Fate, playing the artist, steps in to part the lovers before their feeling for each other dies out completely, before Time alters them, so that perhaps the one may seem "to remain for the other always what he was, / the good-looking young man of twenty-four."

In the city over which the unresurrected Adonis presides, love is apparently doomed to last no more than a passing moment, and the principal recompense for its inevitable frustration and dissolution seems to be the intensity of that moment, a felt pleasure too vital and compelling to be hindered by guilt or diminished by shame. A number of poems underline this theme, portraying protagonists at the hour when they let themselves go, when they "give in completely" to their pleasure, as the poet puts it in an early poem, "I Went" (1905), and again in "Passing Through" (1914). We have already seen such recompense suggested in "Comes to Rest" and "Two Young Men, 23 to 24 Years Old," where the erotic moods conveyed are those of fleshly delight and joy. The motif is repeated in "In the Boring Village" (1925), where the protagonist is described as giving his youth over "to a fine intensity" while finding his pleasure in sleep. The poet's sympathy toward the banishment of all guilt and shame during moments of abandon comes across directly in "He Had Planned to Read" (1924), where the "very good-looking" twenty-three year old who is "completely devoted to books" finds himself unable to read for more than ten minutes, because he is drawn into a daydream of his afternoon's pleasure, when

        . . . Eros penetrated
his ideal flesh, his lips,
an erotic warmth penetrated
his lovely flesh—
with no ridiculous shame about the form the pleasure took . . .

But these moments of abandon in the presence of uninhibited
Eros are rather few in Cavafy's work, and however intense the
pleasures that characterize them, they nevertheless belong to the
unmetamorphosed, transient, and partial world of the poet's
actual city. No relief from the influence of time and fate is possible within the confines of this world; the only true relief, the
only lasting consolation, comes with its transformation into art.
In Cavafy's poetics, art—or the artistic imagination—is given
the function of completing and elevating what is partial and
transitory. It is art that raises the ephemeral and the unrealized,
the shabby and commercial, the passion of momentary ecstasies,
to another region where the mind holds power and sway, the
realm of imaginative re-creation, in short, the world of poetry.
The process is identified by the poet himself in "I've Brought to
Art" (1921):

I sit in a mood of reverie.
I've brought to Art desires and sensations:
things half-glimpsed,
faces or lines, certain indistinct memories
of unfulfilled love affairs.
Let me submit to Art:
Art knows how to shape forms of Beauty,
almost imperceptibly completing life,
blending impressions, blending day with day.

Poetry not only becomes the avenue toward permanence and
completion for that which is transitory and partial; it becomes
the ultimate fulfullment of that which can never be totally fulfilled outside the life of the mind. And it also becomes an exoneration for a kind of love that society considers disreputable and
corrupt.

    This elevation of Cavafy's Sensual City above the transient
passions that inhabit the actual world outside his window depends on two necessary agents of his art: an honest if some-

times indistinct memory, and an honest if sometimes deliberately veiled expression of what he remembers. We have seen memory identified as the agent of several of the experiences that most moved the poet: "quick baring of flesh—a vision / that has crossed twenty-six years / and now comes to rest in this poetry," and "red lips so intoxicating / that now as I write, after so many years, / in my lonely house, I'm drunk with passion again." In fact, most of Cavafy's poems of contemporary Alexandria emerge from reverie, from an experience or image recollected out of a more or less distant past, which is searched as scrupulously as memory permits and is often offered simply for its own sake—a face or figure outlined, an encounter briefly described, a short history narrated—as though the acts of recollection and definition, however incomplete, however sketchy, are poetic acts sufficient in themselves to give a fleeting experience or image the kind of permanence that life in the flesh could never have:

I'd like to speak of this memory,
but it's so faded now—as though nothing's left—
because it was so long ago, in my adolescent years.
A skin as though of jasmine . . .
that August evening—was it August?—
I can still just recall the eyes: blue, I think they were . . .
Ah yes, blue: a sapphire blue.

["Long Ago," 1914]

One is tempted to question whether this seemingly uncomplicated re-creation of the past is a sufficient poetic statement, especially when the details are as conventional as "a skin as though of jasmine" and "sapphire blue" eyes. But it is clear that the force of the poem, the element of drama in it, is intended to reside in the act of recollection itself, in the tension the act arouses: ". . . was it August?— / . . . the eyes: blue, I think they were . . . / Ah yes, blue . . ." This small drama not only heightens the sentiment of the poem but also makes recollection, rather than the specifics of what is recollected, the governing theme: recollection as the redeeming and abiding issue of a long lost passion. The act of recollection is also depicted as a passionate act in itself, with apparent sensual rewards for the poet's persona ("after so many years . . . I'm drunk with passion again"). We are told that recollection is his "life's joy and incense" in the poem appropriately entitled "To Sensual Pleasure" (1913); it is the way to a vicarious reliving of those moments when the persona "found and captured pleasure as I wanted it." But clearly the most important service that memory renders is in intercepting time, in fixing and bringing back what time has altered, so that the original shape of things can be re-created in the poet's art and held there for as long as the poetry has life:

Those gray eyes will have lost their charm—if he's still alive;
that lovely face will have spoiled.
Memory, keep them the way they were.
And, memory, whatever you can bring back of that love,
whatever you can, bring back tonight
                                                    ["Gray," 1917]

If Cavafy's Adonis is doomed to remain unresurrected within the confines of the poet's actual city, it seems that at least a partial resurrection is possible within the elevated realm of imaginative re-creation, where memory rules, as the concluding lines of this poem imply: "memory, whatever you can bring back, . . . bring back tonight." Of course the act of recollection, however honest and complete, is not enough in itself to effect this resurrection, this gift of new life to the dead or dying past: it must result in a re-creation that can pass as a work of art, and the work of art must be promulgated at some point if the exercise (not to say ritual) is to rise above mere self-indulgence. We have seen that it took Cavafy until the age of forty to find the courage —or the need—to come to terms with his past in a way that made possible a candid poetic re-creation of the passions that characterize his image of contemporary Alexandria, and then close to another ten years to discover a mode and a pattern that would provide aesthetic justification for publishing the Sensual City he had created. His discovery in this area coincides, roughly, with the date that he chose to mark his emergence as a mature poet, that is, 1911, though the pattern does not begin to be clearly manifest until several years later. I indicated at the beginning of this chapter that his version of "two-plane writing"—manipulating a continuous parallel between contemporaneity and antiquity by providing juxtaposed images of contemporary and ancient Alexandria—became the mode that justified his delayed revelation in aesthetic terms. A further more personal and philosophical justification, that of past passion resurrected and given permanence by its metamorphosis into art, actually becomes a central theme of his work as the re-created image of contemporary Alexandria gradually emerges, beginning with "Very Seldom," a poem written in 1911 but first published in 1913. The protagonist here, who is a sensualist become "a tattered coat upon a stick" in Yeats's phrase, finds some consolation for the shambles of his old age in the vicarious hold on youth that the poetry he has created out of his indulgence now brings him:

An old man—used up, bent,
crippled by time and indulgence—
slowly walks along the narrow street.
But when he goes inside his house to hide
the shambles of his old age, his mind turns
to the share in youth that still belongs to him.

His verse is now quoted by young men.
His visions come before their lively eyes.
Their healthy sensual minds,
their shapely taut bodies
stir to his perception of the beautiful.

It is difficult to read this poem without seeing Cavafy himself as the old poet entering his house on that narrow street, even if we remember that it would have to be a projection by the poet of a future image of himself, since he was only forty-eight at the time "Very Seldom" was written. We cannot avoid the suspicion that it is exactly that kind of image: what one might call a bit of autobiographical wishful thinking concealed in the third person. In any case, the poet's impulse, and finally his commitment, to give full meaning and some lasting life to the homosexual passions of his contemporary city by re-creating them in his verse comes out clearly in other less indirect poems of this period, especially in three written between 1913 and 1915, when his pattern of revelation was well in progress, albeit in the controlled, still partially hidden, context that ambiguity of gender permitted. In "When They Come Alive" (1913), despite the stratagem of a speaker addressing a listener called "poet," we hear Cavafy addressing himself as he exhorts the poet to keep and hold "those erotic visions of yours" so that they can be put, half-hidden, in his lines. The poem significantly entitled "Understanding" (1915) eliminates all grammatical distance between poet and "poet" by outlining the theme directly and precisely in the first person:

My younger days, my sensual life—
how clearly I see their meaning now.

What needless, futile regret . . .

But I didn't see the meaning of it then.

In the loose living of my early years
the impulses of my poetry were shaped,
the boundaries of my art were plotted.

Guilt and regret are here replaced by understanding. The poet has gained the freedom to exploit all aspects of his Sensual City that can be legitimately exploited for the purposes of his art, and what was loose, illicit, furtive, and morally unacceptable in the past can now find its place in the sun, impelled by honest recollection and the transforming imagination to realize a more lasting life in the country of artifice. The process of redemption is rendered dramatically and objectively in another poem written in the same year, 1915, "Their Beginning":

Their illicit pleasure has been fulfilled.
They get up and dress quickly, without a word.
They come out of the house separately, furtively;
and as they move off down the street a bit unsettled,
it seems they sense that something about them betrays
what kind of bed they've just been lying on.

But what profit for the life of the artist:
tomorrow, the day after, or years later, he'll give voice
to the strong lines that had their beginning here.

It is usually the aging artist exercising his memory "years later" —perhaps as the Proteus that Seferis had in mind—who attempts to redeem a youthful sensuality by giving it expression in poetic form. In "Passing Through" (1914), the first abandon of a "young sensualist with blood fresh and hot," in itself a rather conventional initiation for all its "forbidden erotic ecstasy," changes the protagonist from just "a simple boy" into "something worth our looking at" only when the poet brings the sensualist's new-found pleasure to life again years later in the "exalted World of Poetry." And when the poet tells us in "I've Looked So Much . . ." (1911) that he's looked on beauty so much that his vision now overflows with it, the vision is again that of an older poet reviewing "nights when I was young," re-creating erotic figures that are worthy of being taken out of time, worthy of being saved from mere conventionality ("Red lips. Sensual limbs. / Hair as though stolen from Greek statues") because they appeared "as my poetry desired them." The poem "In the Same Space," quoted earlier, demonstrates that the aging poet's commitment to redeem the city of his youthful passions by transforming it into the "artifice of eternity"—to invoke Yeats's related interest—had become so total and complete by the end of his life (the poem was written in 1929) that he could speak of having *created* the setting of houses and cafés, the neighborhood that he'd seen and walked through years on end, a setting the whole of which had finally been transformed into feeling for him.

The transformation has been at some cost. As one senses that the aging Yeats finds his voyage from the country of the sensual young in one another's arms to the holy city of gold mosaics a harder journey than the rhetoric of "Sailing to Byzantium" makes it seem, so too one senses that Cavafy's voyage from a passionate reality to a redemption in art has been made at a high price. With the elevation of his city to a realm where memory, imagination, and metamorphosed feeling rule entirely, where the act of poetic creation has come to replace the act of involved physical passion, we discern that the actual city outside his window has become unrecognizable to him, in fact, no longer really there at all: literally changed by the passing of time but also made inaccessible by the poet's intense preoccupation with the haunting image of an earlier city:

Half past twelve. Time's gone by quickly
since nine o'clock when I lit the lamp
and sat down here. I've been sitting without reading,
without speaking. Completely alone in the house,
who could I talk to?
Since nine o'clock when I lit the lamp
the shade of my young body

has been haunting me, reminding me
of shut scented rooms,
of past passion—what daring passion.
And it's also brought back to me
streets now unrecognizable,
bustling night clubs now closed,
theatres and cafés no longer there.

[From "Since Nine O'Clock", 1917]

It seems that in the case of both Yeats and Cavafy, the process of redemption, of transient life transformed into permanent art, is a process of alienation as well, one that isolates the poet from the world of flesh and blood—of "whatever is begotten, born, and dies"—that once was the passionate center of his being. All has now become feeling divorced from the possibility of direct contact with the original sources of feeling, all has become life relived in memory only. The obsession with remembered experience is so complete that the poet has to force himself to believe that he really sees even the very rare and momentary glimpses he has of the natural world around him, as in "Morning Sea" (1915), where we find the poet who has focused his vision on the life of city streets these many years (at least since 1904) stopping to "look at nature awhile"—at the "brilliant blue of the morning sea, of the cloudless sky"—only to find that even in a setting "all bathed in light," he is still irresistibly haunted by the same sensual memories and images which have come to dominate his daydreaming imagination so thoroughly that he can really see nothing else:

Let me stand here. And let me pretend I see all this
(I actually did see it for a minute when I first stopped)
and not my usual day-dreams here too,
my memories, those sensual images.

But with the poet's alienation from his present-day world comes not a full release from "those dying generations at their song," as Yeats put it, but a tormenting recognition of what is no longer there, of beauty gone, of the body's aging, of a heart "sick with desire / And fastened to a dying animal." It would seem that the danger of an inspiration so attached to an honest recollection and revelation of past passions is that the more thorough the recollection and the revelation, the more painful

The Sensual City   65

the artist's sense of what time has cost him of the passionate life he is attempting to re-create. His art is a kind of final consolation, but even that consolation appears to be partial in the end—if we can assume that the voice in "Melancholy of Jason Kleander, Poet in Kommagini, A.D. 595," speaks to some degree for Cavafy himself:

The aging of my body and my beauty
is a wound from a merciless knife.
I turn to you, Art of Poetry,
because you have a kind of knowledge about drugs:
certain sedatives, in Language and Imagination.

It's a wound from a merciless knife.
Bring your drugs, Art of Poetry—
they do relieve the pain at least for a while.

The phrase "at least for a while" tells all—including, one senses, some recognition on Cavafy's part of the painful dilemma that apparently arises with his kind of almost ascetic commitment to the artistic re-creation of a life once actually and intensely felt. In Jason Kleander's passionate plea for what he knows can only be a temporary relief in "Language and Imagination," we feel the related passion of the aging Cavafy, wounded by the very images he has created and the sense of loss they bring with them, acknowledging, at least indirectly, that the gods of this Sensual City he has been celebrating are bound to abandon him in the end because they are part and parcel of the streets and cafés, the flesh and blood life, that has some time since begun to recede out of view below his balcony window.

The poet's loss is in one sense the reader's gain. The disappearance of the poet's actual city, however painful its going may seem to the aging sensualist, is not only inevitable but essential for the kind of art created by the practitioner of the Alexandrian mode, the artificer who is out to capture the city represented by the invisible procession of musicians, with its strange and exquisite music, that Cavafy's Antony came to know in his last moments. Actual, literal Alexandria really counts only to the extent that it serves as a catalyst for the creation of a poetic city in its image. We have seen that even in the series of poems that remain closest to the world Cavafy could see outside his balcony window, the poet's imagination, stimulated by memory, plays continually over what he sees so as to transform his actual contemporary Alexandria into a city of remembered sensations, only once actually identified by name,[14] a city rooted in a physical reality that he once knew but that he selectively reshaped, redefined as half real and half wrought by his own mind, in a way idealized, finally dramatized, and elevated to serve the purposes of art. It is this city—the one the poet "created . . . / with so many incidents, so many details" and published with more courage than he has perhaps been credited—that has so far survived the influence of time, an exoneration the poet himself may have anticipated but was not fully able to delight in during his own lifetime.

The phrase "created . . . / with so many incidents, so many details," from the 1929 poem "In the Same Space," suggests that Cavafy may have been aware, by the end of his life, exactly what it was in his mode of creation that served to bring his city of remembered sensations to life: a specificity in the use of details that both undercut an excess of sentiment and particularized emotions that would have otherwise remained vague, nostalgic, sensational merely. We have seen that the poet recognized from the start the virtue of establishing a sense of place in his erotic poetry (for example, in the two "unpublished" poems of 1904, "On the Stairs" and "At the Theater"), but it took him some years to create a sense of reality through concrete detail, once he had begun to publish his image of the Sensual City in 1912, and it was only in some of his later poems that he found proper objective correlatives for the emotion he felt and wished to convey. The first relevant poem, "Come Back" (1904), published in 1912, offers no sense of place, nor much else that is precise, limiting itself to an emotion called "sensation that I love," invoked to return "when lips and skin remember / and hands feel as though they touch again." The second poem in the series, "I Went" (1905), published in 1913, is almost as indefinite, the setting only that of "the brilliant night," the action only that of drinking strong wine "the way the champions of pleasure drink." And the physical descriptions in the poems published during these relatively early years remain consistently general and vague: "A skin as though of jasmine" ("Long Ago," pub. 1914), "those intoxicating lips, / red and sensual" ("One Night," pub. 1915), "The poetic eyes, the pale face, / those lips" ("Days of 1903," pub. 1917). These descriptions are neither specific nor provocative enough to convey an original, particular image, and as a consequence they do not serve very effectively to dramatize and objectify the poet's emotion. Even in his later poems, the terms that define physical beauty are often general and hyperbolic: "the rare beauty of his face . . . / with those ideal lips" ("In an Old Book," 1922), or "his lovely youth given over to a fine intensity" ("In the Boring Village," 1925), or the "exquisite, . . . perfect" ironmonger's assistant in "Days of 1909, '10, and '11" (1928), or the "total beauty" of the tailor's assistant in "The Mirror in the Front Hall" (1930).

But the weakness here, the use of general terms, or rhetorical adjectives, to convey a supposedly heightened sentiment, is compensated for by the poet's specificity in other areas, sometimes within the same poem: a specificity in dress, gesture, setting, and sometimes action. The poet's development in this regard is quite striking, especially when one remembers that he was among the first in recent centuries to explore and describe the forbidden territory of homosexual love.[15] For example, the "tastefully discriminating dress" of "At the Theater," a detail rather precious and undefined, becomes "something of the artist in the way he dresses / —the color of his tie, shape of his collar—" in "In the Street," written nine years later (in 1913); and some fifteen years after that, in "Picture of a 23-Year-Old Painted by his Friend of the Same Age, an Amateur," we find the poet becoming both more precise and more down to earth:

He's painted him wearing an unbuttoned gray jacket,
no vest, tieless,
with a rose-colored shirt,
open, allowing a glimpse
of his beautiful chest and neck.

Finally, in the last poem published during his lifetime, "Days of 1908" (1932), the tastefully discriminating dress has been reduced to a "very faded cinnamon-brown suit" whose only virtue is that it can be thrown off to reveal "mended underwear" and ultimately the "miracle" of a naked body underneath.

We have already encountered, in several of Cavafy's later poems, the kind of specificity in gesture and action that I have in mind, for example, the "quick baring of flesh" in "Comes to Rest" (1918) and the "moment's meeting of limb against limb" in "He Asked about the Quality" (1930). The treatment of sexual activity in these instances is no more overt than what one finds in the Greek Anthology and less ribald than Martial's use of homosexuality, but there are no parallels among homosexual poets in our tradition until much later in the twentieth century. And some contemporary tastes still resist one of the more startling erotic poems that Cavafy wrote, certainly the most avant garde for his time, "The Bandaged Shoulder," written in 1919 and kept among the unpublished material in his archives, probably out of reticence on Cavafy's part. From my point of view, the bloody rag and the persona's gesture toward it seem exactly the kind of efficacious details—so essential to an honest dramatization of erotic sentiment—that are missing from much of his earlier verse: details candid yet retaining enough mystery to nourish the imagination:

I did it [the bandage] up again, taking my time
over the binding; he wasn't in pain
and I liked looking at the blood.
It was a thing of my love, that blood.

When he left, I found, in front of his chair,
a bloody rag, part of the dressing,
a rag to be thrown straight into the garbage;
and I put it to my lips
and kept it there a long while—
the blood of love against my lips.

There is evidence of a related progress in Cavafy's treatment of settings around the time this poem was written. The tavernas represented in "Comes to Rest" and "The Twenty-fifth Year of His Life," both written in 1918, have a degree of character, a felt presence, that create the proper realistic context for the poet's city of remembered sensations, as was not always the case in earlier poems, where the context is often only a setting identified by name or a reference to the city's night. In "The Afternoon Sun," also written in 1918, the focus is almost entirely on context: a detailed description of the room in which the persona and his lover, long since separated, used to meet—before the house became "an office building for agents, businessmen, companies." This focus not only establishes a specific foundation for the poet's reverie; it also saves what would otherwise seem a rather self-indulgent exercise in nostalgia by providing a set of objects—"those old things"—that become the formula of the poet's emotion (to use Eliot's terms): chairs, couch, wardrobe, the table "where he wrote," and especially the bed—half-crossed by sunlight—"where we made love so many times." The bed is reintroduced to offer the right touch of reality at that moment when the poet's feeling begins to move dangerously close to the sentimental:

This room, how well I know it.
Now they're renting it, and the one next to it,
as offices. The whole house has become
an office building for agents, businessmen, companies.

This room, how familiar it is.

The couch was here, near the door,
a Turkish carpet in front of it.
Close by, the shelf with two yellow vases.
On the right—no, opposite—a wardrobe with a mirror.
In the middle the table where he wrote,
and the three big wicker chairs.
Beside the window the bed
where we made love so many times.

They must still be around somewhere, those old things.

Beside the window the bed;
the afternoon sun used to touch half of it.

. . . One afternoon at four o'clock we separated
for a week only . . . And then—
that week became forever.

The change of this house of love into an office building is symbolic of the general disparity between the poet's remembered city and the actual city below his balcony window, that disappearing city with "streets now unrecognizable, . . . theatres and cafés no longer there" which he described in "Since Nine O'Clock," written the previous year. As I have suggested, the disparity is both inevitable and essential, not only because cities do change with time—and sometimes quickly (witness the disparity between pre- and post-Nasser Alexandria)—but because the earlier city has in any case been appropriately transformed by the poet's imagination, by the impulses of his relived passion, and by his cunning selection of details so that it can carry the emotional weight of a central poetic image. It is in fact no less a creation, even at times no less an idealization, than the image of ancient Alexandria that shapes the other plane of Cavafy's parallel between contemporaneity and antiquity.

This is not to suggest that either the creation or the idealization is on the same scale in the two poetic cities. As we shall see, the image of ancient Alexandria encompasses a society, a way of life, an ideology, a broad spread of history, while the image of the later city is largely restricted to a particular erotic world at a prescribed moment in the near-present. But the two planes come close to converging in the poet's imaginative re-creation of the erotic experience that characterizes each. The relationship between the two planes cannot be fully explored until each plane has been described in detail, but it should be pointed out that the relationship is one of analogy, which includes differences as well as similarities, and that it is fairly complex. One might assume that the conception of love that characterizes Cavafy's image of contemporary Alexandria, that of the unresurrected Adonis, is used primarily to make an ironic comparison between the two planes: an occasion for contrasting the furtive, transient, mucky experience of the present with the glories of Ptolemaic and post-Ptolemaic Alexandria. That assumption is not entirely wrong, as we shall see later in the discussion of Cavafy's "ancient epitaphs," but it is an incomplete view. Though there is a clear contrast between the circumstances and social role of lovers in the two cities, a clear difference in how the lovers are viewed by their society and in the value placed upon what they represent, the two planes in general project much the same image of erotic experience itself, especially in terms of the characters and attitudes involved. There is little to choose, for example, between the card player of "Days of 1908" or the drifting go-between of "Days of 1896" on the one hand, and the opportunistic protagonists of "From the School of the Renowned Philosopher" or "Tomb of Iasis" on the other, except a difference in ambitions and social class. It is true—and not insignificant to Cavafy—that the ancient protagonist of "In the Tavernas" loses his lover to the son of a prefect who offers the lover a villa on the Nile, while the contemporary protagonist of "Lovely White Flowers" loses his lover to "a liar, a real bum" who offers the lover a single suit ("and that under pressure"), but the passion and the pain are much the same in these two worlds, and the redeeming element in both is generally the exquisite beauty of the lovers involved, the intensity of the doomed pleasures they knew, and the sustenance that memory provides.

It seems that the major thematic purpose of the parallel between the Sensual Cities of Cavafy's ancient and modern worlds was to underline areas of continuity, even of identity, between past and present in the erotic experience of the lovers portrayed, while at the same time underlining the vast differences between past and present in the station and social roles of these lovers. Put in its simplest terms, the lovers of Cavafy's ancient Alexandria are not only accepted by their society, but are often depicted as representing the best which that society has to offer—the best of the young, anyway—whereas Cavafy's contemporary lovers are generally depicted as impoverished outcasts. And the major technical purpose of the parallel was to provide a level of realism, in both context and language, that would permit the poet (and the reader) to move with easily suspended disbelief from one world to the other: a mode, in short, for making the image of eroticism in Cavafy's ancient Alexandria appear as alive and current as that in the contemporary city of theatres, cafés, brothels, and transient affairs—everything that worked to shape the poet's "memories, those sensual images" into a city of remembered sensations.

The focus does not move merely *from* the contemporary *to* the ancient. There is a movement in both directions: an illumination of the present by its analogy to the past, and vice-versa. And in at least one instance Cavafy uses a direct allusion to his "great Alexandria / of ancient times" in order to highlight a bit of glory in the present:

He was the son of a misused, poverty-stricken sailor
(from an island in the Aegean Sea).
He worked for an ironmonger: his clothes shabby,
his workshoes miserably torn,
his hands filthy with rust and oil.

In the evenings, after the shop closed,
if there was something he longed for especially,
a more or less expensive tie,
a tie for Sunday,
or if he saw and coveted
a beautiful blue shirt in some store window,
he'd sell his body for a half-crown or two.

I ask myself if the great Alexandria
of ancient times could boast of a boy
more exquisite, more perfect—thoroughly neglected though he
   was:
that is, we don't have a statue or painting of him;
thrust into that poor ironmonger's shop,
overworked, harassed, given to cheap debauchery,
he was soon used up.

["Days of 1909, '10, and '11"]

In beauty, this young Adonis of contemporary Alexandria is equal to anything the ancient city could provide; the only difference, the poet would have us believe, is in his circumstances and in the recognition granted him. Where the ancients would have celebrated him with a statue or a painting—and no doubt would have offered him opportunities for debauchery rewarded on the grandest scale—contemporary society, with "all its values wrong" (as he puts it in "Days of 1896"), not only neglects him but apparently uses him up by forcing him to overwork and to give himself to cheap debauchery for the sake of a tie or shirt. The implied socio-political sentiments are perhaps excessive (given the normal range of priorities in the twentieth century, it is difficult to blame even the society of British-occupied Egypt for failing to support this Adonis under some system of patronage that would reward beauty alone), but other implications of the parallel between contemporaneity and antiquity are acceptable enough: Alexandria goes on being Alexandria still in the idols it offers, and what the ancient artist did for such beauty in his day, our poet will do in his through this commemorative poem. It is this work, the poem, that resurrects the lost Adonis of Cavafy's contemporary world: a modern epitaph, if you will, to keep his image alive in the continuing history of exquisite young men who have had their cruel moment in the city our poet loved and who have now passed into "the exalted World of Poetry" to be redeemed from the realities of time.

chapter four

Mythical Alexandria

When Cavafy chose 1911 as the dividing line between his apprenticeship and his maturity—even though he had turned forty-eight in that year[1]—he was signalling a number of things (sometimes more than he might have consciously acknowledged): his accommodation with Alexandria and his total commitment to his muse; his decision to build an image of the Sensual City through a gradual revelation of his erotic proclivities; and, most important of all, the first flowering of a central preoccupation during his mature years: the creation of a mythical city called Alexandria. This preoccupation especially motivated his poetic enterprise during the eleven years between 1911 and 1921, years dominated by poems about ancient Alexandria; but it also helped to shape the Cavafy canon during the late stages of his maturity, when his myth broadened to include a comprehensive Hellenic world—Asia Minor, Syria, Judaea, Libya, Italy—of which Alexandria, and the Greek way of life it represented, remained the center.

As we saw earlier, "The God Abandons Antony" is the poem that introduces Cavafy's mythical ancient city. The poet's primary intention in this poem was to deify the city that gave Antony his best—and some of his worst—days. The deification was manifest first of all in the poet's handling of his historical sources: his substitution of the god Alexandria for Plutarch's Dionysus and Shakespeare's Hercules as the deity that presides over Antony's fate and finally abandons him at his moment of total undoing. It is this city that should represent, in the poet's view, the divine possibility now no longer available to our hero: that special way of life that the Roman had come to worship—had proven worthy of worshipping—a way of life only hinted at in this first evocation, but the subject of poem after poem in the years that followed.

The supreme confidence of the speaker's voice in "The God Abandons Antony," a voice that can tell even the great Roman soldier what his stance should be in his hour of doom, derives from the assumption that the divinity of Alexandria can be taken for granted. The speaker does not say exactly what it is that makes Alexandria divine, that makes it a valid substitute for Dionysus or Hercules. We learn only that Antony has been given "this kind of city" and that his "final pleasure" should be to listen to the exquisite music of the invisible procession that signals the departure of the god he worships. There are hints of an infinite variety of pleasures now gone in the phrase "final pleasure"—hints of what has been called Cavafy's "hedonistic bias"[2]—and the emphasis on "exquisite music" may point to a parallel artistic bias; but that is all we are given within the poem itself. Yet "The God Abandons Antony" succeeds, nevertheless, in projecting the first substantial image of the city at the heart of Cavafy's poetic world during his mature years, and it does so with subtle effectiveness precisely because the mystery of the poem includes a divinity that is left as undefined, as rich in possibilities merely intimated, as a mortal god presumably should be if it is to stir the imagination to the heightened devotion the poem presupposes. And this strategy makes it easy for us to share in the presupposition. The god is given us in the phrase "this kind of city"; the god's attributes, the divine characteristics of the Alexandrian life Antony worshiped, are those our own imagination proposes, stimulated by the theatre of history—what we know of the hero's pleasures as Plutarch and Shakespeare have delineated them—and by the poet's confident rhetoric: "listen—your final pleasure—to the voices, / to the exquisite music of that strange procession, / and say goodbye to her, to the Alexandria you are losing."

A number of the "historical" poems that Cavafy wrote and published during 1911-1921 describe in some detail what the poet means by "this kind of city" and by the figure considered worthy of the gift it represents; in short, they illuminate the images of ancient Alexandria and ancient Alexandrian, whether the latter is a native son or a convert from another country such as Antony.[3] Of the forty-odd "historical" poems that Cavafy published between "The God Abandons Antony" in 1911 and the end of the period in 1921, roughly half are devoted to rendering some aspect of these two images. We can therefore say that during this time the poet's vision was consciously and consistently directed toward the completion of what "The God Abandons Antony" promised, with the main thrust falling in the seven years from 1911 through 1917, when he brought out

Cavafy's Alexandria

twelve of the twenty-six poems of ancient Alexandria that he published in his lifetime.[4]

The detailed characterization of his mythical city begins with "The Glory of the Ptolemies," written and published in 1911 (see p. 23). In this poem, a "hedonistic bias" colors the speaker's monologue from the opening lines: the most important thing— the immediate fruit of power and wealth—is a complete mastery of the art of pleasure. Such mastery becomes the speaker's criterion for claiming superiority over the best that Greek or barbarian can boast of, but in particular over the "cheap" efforts of the Ptolemies' perennial rivals, the Seleucids. Yet Cavafy's arrogantly hedonistic Alexandrian knows there are "other things" that may count for the outside observer indicated by the poem's "you": learning and art, for example. In these the speaker's Alexandria is also supreme, in fact "queen of the Greek world" (or, more literally, "apex of the Greek world"). Who is the speaker making these grand claims? Cavafy is deliberately imprecise: one of the early Lagids, representing the Ptolemaic dynasty, as "son of Selefkos" (or "Selefkides") represents the competing Seleucid dynasty. It is enough to know that we are at a high point in the early history of Alexandria; in fact, the absence of a precise date and a specific historical figure permits the kind of generalized reading that establishes the foundations of the poet's mythical city. Lagides is the archetypal early Alexandrian king; his city, the glory of the Ptolemies, is the essential early Alexandria, center of those preoccupations that best define Cavafy's conception of "our life," as his speaker puts it in "For Ammonis, Who Died at 29, in 610": hedonism, art, learning, and the celebration of Hellenism, especially the Greek language. These are the elements that gradually shape, through reiteration, the ideal Alexandria of Cavafy's poems. They become the ideology of that special life that unites Alexandrians through the ages, from the days of Ptolemy I Soter in the fourth century B. C. to the time of Ammonis in the seventh century A. D. And to know the value of that life, whether Lagid king, Roman general, or Egyptian poet, is to live as close to mortal glory as one can in the world Cavafy created.

Hedonism dominates the shaping elements of Cavafy's myth.

There is hardly a poem about ancient Alexandria that is not colored by the poet's "hedonistic bias," and when hedonism comes into conflict with some other compelling impulse, the lust after pleasure inevitably carries the day. In "Dangerous Thoughts" (1911), for example, though the danger alluded to in the title remains unspecified in the poem, the implication is that it resides in the assumption of the young—and presumably unacclimated—Syrian who has come to study in Alexandria during the fourth century A. D. that he will be able to recover his ascetic spirit by an exercise of will power after having committed himself passionately to the pursuit of sensual pleasures. The evidence, as Cavafy sees it, points to the contrary: when one has sampled the fleshpots of his Alexandria, no amount of meditation, study, or resolution is likely to make the will strong enough to restore any competing impulse. The attitude, the bias, is made explicit in "Of the Jews (A.D. 50)" (1919), where even the ties of birth, family, and religion are insufficient against the pull of Alexandrian sensuality:

Painter and poet, runner, discus-thrower,
beautiful as Endymion: Ianthis, son of Antony.
From a family on close terms with the Synagogue.

"My most valuable days are those
when I give up the pursuit of sensuous beauty,
when I desert the elegant and severe cult of Hellenism,
with its over-riding devotion
to perfectly shaped, corruptible white limbs,
and become the man I would want to remain forever:
son of the Jews, the holy Jews."

A most fervent declaration on his part: ". . . to remain forever
a son of the Jews, the holy Jews."

But he didn't remain anything of the kind.
The Hedonism and Art of Alexandria
kept him as their dedicated son.

Though a son of the Jews, the protagonist has a Greek name, and his attributes make him eminently qualified for the Hellenic way of life; he is artistic, athletic, beautiful, fervent. And he is obviously easy bait for the particular kind of Hellenic cult his father's namesake knew. The cult is indeed severe (or "hard":

σκληϱόν); once one has begun to worship the god Alexandria, there is apparently no turning back. And the worship breeds excess. We are given the impression that for all the elegance and beauty, for all the variety of sensual delight this god represents, there is a pernicious aspect to him; he not only demands a relentless, hard devotion, but what he demands can kill:

I, Iasis, lie here—famous for my good looks
in this great city.
the wise admired me, so did common, superficial people.
I took equal pleasure in both.
But from being considered so often a Narcissus and Hermes,
excess wore me out, killed me. Traveler,
if you're an Alexandrian, you won't blame me.
You know the pace of our life—its fever, its absolute devotion to
    pleasure.

The poem is called "Tomb of Iasis," one of five Alexandrian "epitaphs" that Cavafy published between 1914 and 1918. Each of these has its particular emphasis, but the five poems share characteristics that serve to build a composite image—one that seems, when the poems are reviewed in series, to have been projected intentionally. To begin with, no one of the five depicts a precisely designated moment in history, though we discern from the context in each case that ancient Alexandria is the setting. This lack of specificity again permits a generalized reading that unites the five poems and promotes a composite symbolism. Each commemorates the death of a young man who is directly identified with Alexandria, and in some cases the identification is a crucial aspect of the poem's theme. What the five young protagonists share, besides an early grave, is some degree of fame as the objects of love, usually what might be called an Alexandrian kind of love, which places a premium on physical beauty or its trappings, both being expected to meet the highest standards and both the agents of doom. We have seen that Iasis was "famous" for his good looks in Alexandria and apparently died from the excess compelled by too much admiration. The "epitaph" for Evrion ("Tomb of Evrion," 1914) tells us that the really precious thing about this twenty-five year old Alexandrian was not the historical study that he wrote, but "his form—/ like a vision of

Apollo," now lost forever. Ignatios-Kleon of "Tomb of Ignatios" (1917) reports that he was "famous in Alexandria / (where they're not easily dazzled)" for his houses, gardens, horses, chariots, jewels, and silks—all relegated to oblivion when the protagonist finally "came to his senses" at the end of his twenty-eight years and found ten happy months "in the peace, the security of Christ." And Lanis of "Tomb of Lanis" (1918), perhaps the proudest Alexandrian of all, still shows "what was valuable in him, / something of what [Markos] used to love" in the one relique (of that love) that has survived, a portrait depicting the beauty that Lanis wouldn't permit the portrait painter to exploit as Hyacinth or anyone else but only as what it was, presumably the best of possible manifestations: "Lanis, son of Rametichos, an Alexandrian." Finally, what seems to emerge from the poet's admittedly obscure reconstruction of a fragmentary (and imaginary) ancient epitaph to Lefkios of "In the Month of Athyr" (1917) is not only the stated implication that he was greatly loved by his sorrowing friends, but the unstated implication that to be so greatly loved in an Alexandria so absolutely devoted to pleasure is to court an early death. The poem ends:

I think Lefkios must have been greatly loved.
In the month of Athyr Lefkios went to sleep.

There is no moral judgement in this conclusion, only grounds for pathos. Each of these beautiful young men seems a victim necessarily sacrificed to the god Antony worshiped. In a city where the pursuit of beauty, of "perfectly shaped, corruptible white limbs," is an "over-riding devotion" (as the speaker put it in "Of the Jews"), it is dangerous to walk the streets "like a vision of Apollo," and Cavafy implies that the victim is to be mourned without being blamed. But the city is also not to be blamed. To have been young, beautiful, famous for riches among the not easily dazzled, proud to the point of hubris, and above all greatly loved, may have been to court doom without knowing it, but it is also to have lived the best life of all at the highest degree of intensity, "our life," the life of an Alexandrian. And if the price for such a life is sometimes an early death, a wearing out through excess (even for the Christian convert, granted a mere ten months of peace and security), there is some consolation for the devoted sensualist, even after that life has left him, in the epitaph his beauty earns. The epitaph is important in several ways; it commemorates not only the "divine gift" of the god's victim, but also the quality of the victim's devotion, his abiding faith in the virtue of being Alexandrian, whether or not he explictly acknowledges it—and he usually does.

The character and function of the Cavafian epitaph is most clearly revealed in "For Ammonis, Who Died at 29, in 610" (1917), which has the writing of an epitaph for its subject, an epitaph to commemorate an Egyptian Alexandrian poet named Ammonis who died just before the Arab conquest of Egypt:

Raphael, they're asking you to write a few lines
as an epitaph for the poet Ammonis:
something very tasteful and polished. You can do it,
you're the one to write something suitable
for the poet Ammonis, our Ammonis.

Of course you'll speak about his poems—
but say something too about his beauty,
about that subtle beauty we loved.

Your Greek is always elegant and musical.
But we want all your craftsmanship now.
Our sorrow and our love move into a foreign language.
Pour your Egyptian feeling into the Greek you use.

Raphael, your verses, you know, should be written
so they contain something of our life within them,
so the rhythm, so every phrase clearly shows
that an Alexandrian is writing about an Alexandrian.

The poem focuses on the difference between a conventional and a particular epitaph. The speaker is soliciting lines from a poet named Raphael not just for another poet named Ammonis, but for "our" Ammonis. What is to be commemorated requires a particular craftsmanship and a particular approach, because the epitaph is to serve as a monument to an instance of Cavafy's favorite elegiac subject: a young, beautiful, greatly loved Alexandrian; and the epitaph is also to serve as a monument to that special kind of life that Ammonis represented. Typically, we are not told just what constituted this life; its attributes are to be inferred from the solicited epitaph, from what is regarded as "suitable" for "our Ammonis": something "tasteful and polished," in elegant, musical Greek, something that honors his poems, something that celebrates the "subtle beauty we loved," something that will carry over "Egyptian feeling" into the foreign language (Greek) chosen as the medium for the epitaph, and, finally, something that will convey what all these in effect define: "our" Alexandrian life. Taste, polish, and elegance are the qualities of style to be sought; artistic (poetic) talent and beauty are the attributes to be celebrated; love is the governing preoccupation to be memorialized; feeling is the juice of life to be poured (or "spent" in a sexual sense, one meaning of χύσε) at the moment of commemoration—these are the elements that the epitaph should contain if the reader is to know that an Alexandrian is writing about an Alexandrian. And the quality of being Alexandrian—of being a member of the select, hedonistic, artistic, Philhellenic, if physically and morally expensive, society that this epitaph is to dramatize, along with the others written during this period—is what Cavafy's poem itself finally celebrates.

The relation between this partly mythical ancient society and Cavafy's image of contemporary Alexandria can be clarified further by comparing this poem, and the other "ancient" epitaphs of the decade, with "Days of 1909, '10, and '11," that "modern epitaph" commemorating a characteristic citizen of the poet's contemporary Sensual City (see chapter 2). In place of elegance and riches—those "marvelous houses and gardens, . . / the jewels and silks" that Ignatios knew—the modern figure is pictured as having been worked to death in an ironmonger's shop, ". . . his clothes shabby, / his workshoes miserably torn, / his hands filthy with rust and oil," and his taste in riches satisfied, as best it could be, by "a more or less expensive tie" or "a beautiful blue shirt" that he picked up occasionally after selling his body for "a half-crown or two." There is no style, art, love, or even feeling in the life commemorated in "Days of 1909, '10, and '11." In place of these we are shown a life "overworked, harassed, given to cheap debauchery," finally "used up." This is excess of a rather different kind from that which wore out the too-much admired and too pleasure-loving Iasis. In fact, the analogy to

Cavafy's ancient city in this instance rests on one similarity alone: the exquisite beauty of the young man the poet has chosen to commemorate:

I ask myself if the great Alexandria
of ancient times could boast of a boy
more exquisite, more perfect—thoroughly neglected though he
    was:
that is, we don't have a statue of painting of him;

We don't, of course, because this is Alexandria A. D. 1909-11 rather than the Alexandria of Lanis and Ammonis. Far from sharing a devotion to the beauty eulogized in these lines, the society of Cavafy's contemporary Alexandria thoroughly neglects it: no statue or painting commissioned for a relique, no epitaph solicited for a monument. The only memorial this boy's beauty earns is an unsolicited, nameless one from a poet who appears to be a displaced devotee living out of sympathy with his own time (this sense, and the dubious implication that society is somehow at fault for not having rewarded beauty appropriately, create a tone of excessive pity that rather sentimentalizes the poem). One feels here an undercurrent of lingering bitterness against the society that inhibited the poet in his early experience of Alexandria, the society responsible for the line "I hate the people here and they hate me" in the first draft of "The City," and for the comment "what trouble, what a burden small cities are—what lack of freedom" in his 1907 note on Alexandria.[5] This contrast between his ancient and modern cities highlights the element of nostalgia, of longing for a lost paradise, that clearly led the poet to search for material in the glory of the Ptolemies and the ancient Alexandrian days thereafter. And the effectiveness of this search may help explain Cavafy's continuing accommodation to the "burden small cities are . . . for a man like me—so different" in the years after he began to create an ancient Alexandria of the imagination to complement his image of the grubbier, less creative, more hostile city below his balcony window.

But for a mind like Cavafy's, even paradise is a relative condition, subject to the human limitations of those who experience it.

And as a poetic image, it has to be rendered plausibly, realistic-
ally (not to say cynically), open to whatever complicated attitude the poet's perception dictates. There are hints in these
"ancient" epitaphs that the society of Cavafy's mythical Alexandria, for all its tolerance of, its celebration of, beautiful hedonistic young men and their sometimes reckless love affairs, is not
always so tolerant in other ways. We come away from these
poems with a premonition that is at least partially fulfilled by
later Alexandrian poems, namely, that a society that lives at
such a fevered pace, that boasts of a superiority in all knowledge and art, that breeds above all a pride in itself, is likely to be
intolerant of those of its own who cannot keep up with its demands and those outsiders who try to break into its charmed circle with inadequate credentials or with too little audacity and
craft. Such a society is also likely, in the long run, to wear itself
out, or to become so sated and inbred that an invasion of barbarians, or so-called barbarians, proves to be the inevitable solution. The first hint of this dark side of Cavafy's image, a hint that
ancient Alexandria may be too demanding for its own good,
comes into the plea by Iasis in his epitaph: "Traveler, / if you're
an Alexandrian, you won't blame me. / You know the pace of
our life—its fever, its absolute devotion to pleasure." The key
words here are "fever" ($\vartheta έρμην$) and "absolute" (or "supreme":
$ὑπερτάτη$), which suggest a consuming, relentless, in the end fa-
tally exhausting, mode of life ("excess wore me out, killed me").
A second hint emerges from "Tomb of Ignatios," where we are
shown an Alexandria "not easily dazzled," in this case specifically by riches but one suspects by almost anything—anyway,
an Alexandria that Kleon-Ignatios ultimately rejects so thoroughly that he wishes his twenty-eight years as a "famous" citizen of that city completely "wiped out" and replaced by his ten
months of peace and security in Christ. The discovered "peace"
and "security" suggest that the life abandoned by Kleon-Ignatios
is the same life of feverish insecurity that Iasis knew before
excess wore him out.

Another perspective on the dark side of Cavafy's image is provided by a kind of pseudo epitaph of this period, "Aimilianos
Monai, Alexandrian, A.D. 628-655" (1918), "pseudo" because

the speaker's monologue—the body of the poem—occurs before his death and is followed by an epilogue from the poet that could pass for an epitaph, albeit a rather ironic one. What we find in the monologue is another interpretation of the " σκληρόν " aspect of the Hellenistic cult identified in "Of the Jews, A.D. 50," a harshness that includes malice and calls for the armor of deception:

Out of talk, appearance, and manners
I'll make an excellent suit of armor;
and in this way I'll face malicious people
without the slightest fear or weakness.

They'll try to injure me. But of those
who come near me none will know
where to find my wounds, my vulnerable places,
under the deceptions that will cover me.

So boasted Aimilianos Monai.
One wonders if he ever made that suit of armor.
Anyway, he didn't wear it long.
At the age of twenty-seven, he died in Sicily.

The Alexandria of this poem seems—at least as seen through the eyes of Aimilianos Monai—close to that which Cavafy projected in the first draft of "The City" and in "Hidden Things" (written in 1908 but not published during the poet's lifetime), where he speaks of the obstacles that were distorting the "manner of my life," of "unnoticed actions" and "veiled writing," which alone will allow him to be understood, and of his hope for "a more perfect society" where "someone else made just like me" will be permitted to "act freely." The deceptions of Aimilianos Monai appear rather bolder, and the vicious elements in his society, with its "malicious people" out to "injure" him, rather more threatening; but the poet, approaching the subject in 1918 rather than 1908, is able to write the epilogue with a gentle irony that might have been impossible for him before his adjustment to Alexandria (see chapter 2): he wonders if Aimilianos ever made good on his boast. In any case, whether or not Aimilianos successfully frustrated the malicious elements in his Alexandria becomes a fairly academic question when we review the speaker's dates (A.D. 628-655), since the whole of Alexandrian society was overrun by the Arab Conquest of 641 and was already being transformed during the period indicated in the poem's title, with Aimilianos himself displaced at some point to Sicily, where his suit of armor, if he ever did make it, presumably became rather less relevant. Both Aimilianos and his Alexandria are thus swept aside by the pattern of history implicit in the poet's myth, in this instance not by barbarians but by Moslems bringing a culture alien to Alexandrian Hellenism and a new religion meaning "submission to God."

The one element of ancient Alexandrian society that escapes all traces of authorial qualification or irony, and that apparently survives even cataclysmic historical change, is the passionate Alexandrian devotion to the Greek language. We saw that even as late as A.D. 610 an Egyptian Alexandrian advising a Coptic poet would naturally recommend Greek—though a "foreign language"—as the proper language for demonstrating in verse that an Alexandrian was writing about an Alexandrian. And in the one poem we have dealing with Alexandria after the Arab Conquest, "Exiles" (written in 1914), ninth century exiles read lines by the fifth century Egyptian-Greek poet Nonnos with full enthusiasm, though their reading takes place in an Alexandria that has become much smaller than it was before the Arab Conquest and that has "only a few other Greeks / still left in the city" to carry the language forward. Even when the poet allows Alexandria to be roundly condemned by an outsider for its snobbery, it is the Alexandrian attitude toward the Greek language that exonerates the city, as in the late poem "A Prince from Western Libya," where the unfortunate prince

. . . assumed a Greek name, dressed like the Greeks,
learned to behave more or less like a Greek;
and all the time he was terrified he'd spoil
his reasonably good image
by coming out with barbaric howlers in Greek
and the Alexandrians, in their usual way,
would start to make fun of him, vile people that they are.

Their vileness resides at least partly in their insistence that pretenders to Alexandrian Hellenism know their Greek; and this aspirant, even while condemning them, submits to their demanding standard in language by limiting himself maddeningly "to a few words, / terribly careful of his syntax and pronunciation"—maddening because this forces him to keep "so much talk bottled up inside him."

'Ελληνίζειν—to speak the language of the Greeks—gave Hellenism its name and identified the most significant of its governing principles in the vast spread of territory and time that the term covers, as the historian in Cavafy not only recognized but dramatized when he turned the theme into verse:

We the Alexandrians, the Antiochians,
the Selefkians, and the countless
other Greeks of Egypt and Syria,
and those in Media, and Persia, and all the rest:
with our far-flung supremacy,
our flexible policy of judicious integration,
and our Common Greek Language
which we carried as far as Bactria, as far as the Indians.
[from "In the Year 200 B.C."]

It was "our Common Greek Language" that not only gave some coherence to the world shared by Greeks after Alexander the Great, but held together the diverse, multiracial corner of this world represented in Cavafy's mythical city. Pagan and Christian, Egyptian and Jew, whatever the persuasion, citizens of Cavafy's Alexandria give due honor to the Greek language as "the vehicle of fame"[6] regardless of their particular station or historical milieu (as do the citizens of his Hellenic world in general). And if the Hedonism and Art of Alexandria that captured Ianthis, son of the Jews, in A.D. 50 seems to have lost its specifically Hellenic definition by the time of Raphael and Ammonis in A.D. 610, the art and hedonism of the last years before the Arab Conquest—essentially unchanged in style—are still designated by the Egyptian speaker to receive their commemoration in the traditional language of Hellenistic Alexandria.[7]

The long reign of the Greek language as prince of culture in the mixed society of Alexandria, and the vast sources in Greek constituting the two famous Alexandrian libraries, are what served to make the city "the greatest preceptor" ("διδάσκαλος") of the Greek world for some centuries after Lagides' boast in

"The Glory of the Ptolemies" (see p. 23). The poems we have been considering reflect the city's reputation as the center of learning, but Cavafy's Alexandrians are much less devoted to scholarship than to the life of the senses, and the poet's images of learning are often colored by his hedonistic bias. Evrion, for example, did write "a history / of the province of Arsinoites," yet we are told that this surviving relique cannot make up for the loss of "what was really precious" about him, his physical form. There is no mention of learning in the epitaphs to those beautiful, adored young men Iasis, Lanis, and Lefkios; and Ignatios becomes a lector—for what small learning that signifies—late in his short life and outside Alexandria. Ianthis, Raphael, and Ammonis are all poets, but we have no indication of their having other intellectual interests (the latter two belong, in any case, to a period long after the destruction of the second great library). And Myrtias, identified specifically as a "Syrian student / in Alexandria" who is given to meditation and study, becomes most convincing not when he declares—dangerous thoughts, as we saw—that he will recover his ascetic spirit whenever he wishes, but when he declares that he will give himself without fear "to the most audacious erotic desires, / to the lascivious impulses of my blood." "Herodis Attikos" (1912) provides us with the one fairly general and objective scene of the διδάσκαλος in action, this during the second century A.D., and again the image that emerges is mixed, one part sophistry, one part eros:

. . . young men now in Alexandria,
in Antioch or Beirut
(being trained by Hellenism as its future orators),
meeting at choice banquets
where the talk is sometimes about fine sophistry,
sometimes about their exquisite love affairs,

It is clear that Cavafy's beautiful young men take their learning lightly, whether under the influence of "the greatest preceptor" or otherwise. And in general, his Alexandrians find their principal pleasures—and often their principal careers—not so much in the service of learning as in the service of love, at least for as long as their good looks last. The prototypical case history of an Alexandrian "intellectual"—one who brings together the various possibilities open to him, sorts them out in terms of probable pleasure and profit, and puts them in the perspective most true to Cavafy's image of post-Ptolemaic Alexandria—is in a poem whose title, "From the School of the Renowned Philosopher" (1921), turns out to be a gently ironic comment on some of the pretensions of Lagides, at least with reference to the experience of this characteristic third-century protagonist:

For two years he studied with Ammonios Sakkas,
but he was bored by both philosophy and Sakkas.

Then he went into politics.
But he gave that up. The Prefect was an idiot,
and those around him solemn, officious nitwits:
their Greek—poor fools—barbaric.

After that he became
vaguely curious about the Church: to be baptized
and pass as a Christian. But he soon
let that one drop: it would certainly have caused a row
with his parents, ostentatious pagans,
and right away they would have stopped—
something too horrible to contemplate—
their extremely generous allowance.

But he had to do something. He began to haunt
the corrupt houses of Alexandria,
every secret den of debauchery.

Here he was fortunate:
he'd been given an extremely handsome figure.
and he enjoyed the divine gift.

His looks would last
at least another ten years. And after that?
Maybe he'll go back to Sakkas.
Or if the old man has died meanwhile,
he'll find another philosopher or sophist:
there's always someone suitable around.

Or in the end he might possibly return
even to politics—commendably remembering
the traditions of his family,
duty toward the country,
and other resonant banalities of that kind.

The philosopher to whose "school" the handsome young man of this poem belonged—the Sakkas (or Saccas) he finds so boring—is the famous "Socrates of Neoplatonism" who is reputed to have had Longinus, Plotinus, and the two Origens among his disciples. But if in his old age Sakkas fails to inspire, so does almost everything else. Philosophy is as boring as Sakkas. Politics won't do, because of the solemnity, officiousness, and barbaric Greek of those one has to work with, that is, if one is an Alexandrian given to the unsolemn, casual, and Greek-loving life we have seen in other poems of this period. The Christian Church stirs a momentary interest in this less-than-ostentatious pagan, but matters of religious belief or ritual are never to be taken so seriously as to jeopardize what is really important: the generous allowance that permits the good life. And the good life, an occupation that brings distraction and pleasure rather than remuneration, comes down to the pursuit of Eros in the corrupt houses and secret dens of debauchery that the poet himself came to know in his day some six hundred years later. In any case, all but this kind of activity, with its possibility of enjoying, at least for a while, the "divine gift" of physical beauty, seems a waste of the one talent that really counts as far as this protagonist is concerned—counts, that is, until his looks begin to fade and he has no other choice. And when that day arrives, the one thing no committed Alexandrian permits himself—as the poet told Antony—is any self-deception. Our protagonist implies that going back to "school," whether with Sakkas or some other equally "suitable" philosopher or sophist, is primarily a matter of putting up the right front, presumably for the benefit of those ostentatiously pagan parents. And if it has to be politics, at least he will go into that low enterprise with no illusions that he is professing anything more than the necessary "resonant banalities."

"The greatest preceptor" of Lagides' day has obviously become a bit old and tired by the third century A.D., easily dismissed by the Alexandrian "student" of these pagan-Christian times, a convenience now more than an inspiration. And the chauvinism of Lagides' boast, beginning as it does with an evocation of his family name and ending with its encomium to the city, has become merely a source of banalities. In general, Cavafy's image of the third century suggests a certain world-weariness, an *ennui* of the spirit, that is quite in contrast to the rhetorical flamboyance of the city's earliest spokesman in Cavafy's verse. Yet Alexandria goes on being Alexandria still when it comes to the pleasures of the flesh and the value placed on "the divine gift." The hedonistic bias of Cavafy's image was first made explicit, after all, in "The Glory of the Ptolemies," which opens not with a eulogy to the city's intellectual life—that comes in among "other things"—but with a boast about the same first things that attract our third century protagonist: Lagides' complete mastery of "the art of pleasure," specifically sensual pleasure (though not, he insists, the "cheap lechery" of Selefkides).

The political realism—or, if you will, cynicism—of "From the School of the Renowned Philosopher" is also the logical extension of an attitude that colored the Cavafian image from the beginning—at least in regard to the later Ptolemies—and that continued to color his view of Hellenistic and Byzantine history throughout his mature years. This attitude is first applied to Alexandria in the 1912 poem, "Alexandrian Kings," where we find a comprehensive portrait of the typical Alexandrian "man in the street" of the first century B.C.; he is more responsive, more easily entertained, but—when it comes to insight about the character of politics—only slightly less cynical than our third-century Alexandrian:

The Alexandrians turned out in force
to see Cleopatra's children,
Kaisarion and his little brothers,
Alexander and Ptolemy,
who'd been taken out to the Gymnasium for the first time,
to be proclaimed kings there
before a brilliant array of soldiers.

Alexander: they declared him
king of Armenia, Media, and the Parthians.
Ptolemy: they declared him
king of Cilicia, Syria, and Phoenicia.
Kaisarion was standing in front of the others,
dressed in pink silk,
on his chest a bunch of hyacinths,
his belt a double row of amethysts and sapphires,
his shoes tied with white ribbons
prinked with rose-colored pearls.

They declared him greater than his brothers,
they declared him King of Kings.

The Alexandrians knew of course
that this was all just words, all theatre.

But the day was warm and poetic,
the sky a pale blue,
the Alexandrian Gymnasium
a complete artistic triumph,
the courtiers wonderfully sumptuous,
Kaisarion all grace and beauty
(Cleopatra's son, blood of the Lagids);
and the Alexandrians thronged to the festival
full of enthusiasm, and shouted acclamations
in Greek, and Egyptian, and some in Hebrew,
charmed by the lovely spectacle—
though they knew of course what all this was worth,
what empty words they really were, these kingships.

    The surface action takes place on two planes simultaneously:
on the one plane, the political "theatre" presented by those in
power to impress themselves, their subjects, and perhaps their
rivals in Rome (though the Romans in question, according to
Cavafy's source, Plutarch, saw the event as theatrical and arrogant, an occasion to evince their hatred[8]); and, on the other
plane, the less obvious theatre presented by the Alexandrians in
response to their rulers. Behind these performances is hidden the
truth, which, according to the poet, is known by all participants,
rulers and ruled alike, in this case the fact that "these kingships," proclaimed by Antony and Cleopatra in the Alexandrian
Gymnasium, are empty words, signifying a distribution of territory not sufficiently under control to justify the claims the titles
herald, nor ever likely to be. The Alexandrians of Antony's days
are no less perceptive about certain "banalities" of politics than
Sakkas' former pupil was. And they are equally capable of
putting up a front when required. The difference is in the vitality
of their performance as spectators to the political show
presented them and in the large residue of civic pride that survives their knowledge of the true ways of the world. In place of
the broad-ranging cynicism of Sakkas' pupil, we encounter in
these spectators a brilliant representation of Alexandrian enthu-
siasms under the later Ptolemies. The hedonistic bias is there,
rather muted, in the attention they give Kaisarion's "grace and

Cavafy's Alexandria

beauty"; the artistic bias in their celebration of the Gymnasium as "a complete artistic triumph." And the chauvinism that Sakkas' pupil mocked is still sufficiently alive to permit a parenthetical allusion to Kaisarion's Lagid blood. But what dominates the response of these Alexandrians—what holds together the three principal groups that constitute the city's cosmopolitan citizenry —is their shared love of spectacle on a bright Mediterranean day. It is the "poetic" quality of the sky, the "wonderfully sumptuous" courtiers, the "brilliant array" of soldiers, and the charming dress of Kaisarion that inspire a united enthusiasm. Those acclamations in Greek, Egyptian, and Hebrew, shouted in response to a display of power that no one really believes in at all, are in fact a tribute to the Alexandrian love of theatre, especially the kind of spectacular that evokes their lavish ancestry and requires their own gay participation as bit actors in the crowd.

Cavafy's treatment of this political occasion is characteristic of his "historical" mode in dealing with familiar events; he slants, or extends, or re-creates selective aspects of his historical sources so as to permit his own interpretation of the material and, often, a view of that material from the perspective of someone who is affected by the actions of the mighty but who has only his own cunning or irony for self defense—the ordinary citizen who is easily translated into the "hypocrite lecteur." The game of nations interests Cavafy primarily because of what it reveals about basic, perennial attitudes or emotions and only secondarily because of what it reveals about the historical process— another reflection of his own artistic bias during these years. And his sympathies are consistently with the underdogs, the victims of history rather than its manipulators. In this poem he ignores Antony entirely and refers to Cleopatra only in connection with her children[9]; the focus is on those being manipulated by the event, whether the children receiving their empty titles or the spectators responding to the theatrical performance arranged by the mighty to impress the mighty most of all.

It is this interest in the more accessibly human—as distinct from the grandly political—aspects of history that led Cavafy to concentrate often on those moments in the game of nations involving personal and political defeat, when even the mighty are subject to the manipulation of others still mightier or, ultimately, of a fate beyond their control. The pattern was established by "The God Abandons Antony" and its image of the great Roman soldier at the hour when his luck is failing and his plans are all proving deceptive. Besides "Alexandrian Kings," two other poems of this decade deal with first-century B.C. Alexandria, and these extend the pattern of defeat in related ways. "Kaisarion" (1918) focuses again on the figure Cavafy found the most appealing and the most victimized of Cleopatra's offspring, with the poet himself acting the responsive admirer within the poem. It opens with a bit of irony about the grand family tradition of the Ptolemies, as depicted in a volume of inscriptions the poet has been browsing through:

The lavish praise and flattery are much the same
for each of them. All are brilliant,
glorious, mighty, benevolent;
everything they undertake is full of wisdom.
As for the women of their line, the Berenices and Cleopatras,
they too, all of them, are marvelous.

Confronted with so much glory and might and benevolence, the poet naturally finds himself drawn to "a brief / insignificant mention of King Kaisarion," that last and least mighty of the Ptolemaic line, and, giving his biases full reign, he evokes a vision of this doomed young man to entertain himself in the fading light:

I made you good-looking and sensitive.
My art gives your face
a dreamy, appealing beauty.
And so completely did I imagine you
that late last night,
as my lamp went out—I let it go out on purpose—
I thought you came into my room,

The apparition is Kaisarion in his last moments, "pale and weary, ideal in [the] grief" occasioned by those in command of his fate: the counselors to Octavian who have succeeded in obtaining his execution so as to preclude his becoming a rival to Octavian's grand ambitions. The poem has a double thrust in its re-creation of history: the poet's attempt to solicit sympathy for this doomed—and generally ignored—victim of a political "progress" beyond his control, and the poet's implicit statement about the characterization of the Ptolemies that he discovers in the inscriptions mentioned in the opening stanza. The evocation of Kaisarion's pathetic last hours—signalling the cruel end of the Ptolemaic line—in effect places the unreservedly glorified history of the inscriptions in proper perspective. But it is the poet's intense personalization of his historical material that dominates the poem, excessively for some tastes, since the rhetoric is colored not so much by the pathos of Kaisarion's predicament as by the poet's uninhibited involvement in his late evening vision.

The other poem of this period dealing with the first century B.C, "Theodotos" (1915), focuses on a historical moment prior to the Antony-Cleopatra cycle that so preoccupied the poet in these years. The presence of Alexandria in the poem might seem of no consequence to the poet's intention, in what he himself designated a "symbolic" work, were it not for the following line in the poet's note on the poem, quoted by Malanos and Lechonites: "Alexandria means happiness, success,"[10] that is, symbolic setting for the moment of highest danger in the Cavafian myth. The political context here is the victory of Julius Caesar over Pompey at Pharsalus, which is cause for the elation and sense of triumph that Caesar's arrival in Alexandria confirms, at least until the sudden appearance there of "miserable" Pompey's head on a platter, which gives—or should give—even this thoroughly honored and eminent member of the "truly elect" occasion to question his superiority, to ponder his rise at the expense of others (what Cavafy's note calls "treading on corpses"), and perhaps to anticipate his own ultimate fate. The "triumph" of the mighty is finally as subject to the will of the gods and the hungry ambitions of rival contenders for power as is the mock-triumph of lesser men crowned with the hollow title "King of Kings," or even the lowly happiness of the neighbor next door:

And don't be too sure that in your life—
restricted, regulated, prosaic—
spectacular and horrible things like that don't happen.
Maybe this very moment Theodotos—
bodiless, invisible—
enters some neighbor's tidy house
carrying an equally repulsive head.

The poet's strategy of making his myth appear relevant to the experience of the contemporary reader by presenting the historical moment from the perspective of the perennial average citizen here takes the more direct form of bringing the "hypocrite lecteur," with his "restricted, regulated, prosaic" life, into the poem itself as a potential observer of his neighbor's (and by extension his own) access to sudden spectacular horror.[11]

The lesson that Julius Caesar learns in Cavafy's Alexandria of the first century B.C. is related to the lesson his envoys from Alexandria learned in Delphi a little over a century earlier, during the dispute between Ptolemy VI Philometer and his brother, Ptolemy VIII Evergetis, a moment in the history of Alexandrian kings that inspired two poems during the decade 1911-1921. In "Envoys from Alexandria" (1918), a diplomatic mission to the Delphic oracle to discover which brother is to emerge victorious from the dispute—both having sent lavish gifts—proves irrelevant, because the Alexandrian envoys learn, before the Delphic priests have finished debating "the family affairs of the Lagids," that the oracle they're seeking has already been pronounced in Rome, where disputes among the Ptolemies are now settled by the Roman Senate. It is a wry comment on the decline in glory of the Ptolemaic dynasty, though entirely in keeping with the Cavafian principles that power is inevitably relative, that the average citizen and the mighty alike are subject to the will of others mightier, and that it is hubris to consider your fate a matter entirely open to your own manipulation, even when you feel you've reached the summit of power. But in the other poem on the same historical moment, "The Displeasure of Selefkidis" (1916), the poet—typically—makes use of this same humiliating occasion for a very different kind of wry comment: not on the decline of the Ptolemies but on their political shrewdness—especially by comparison with their rivals, the Seleucids. In this poem, Dimitrios Selefkidis, himself a hostage to the Romans, becomes greatly distressed on learning that Ptolemy VI has arrived in Rome dressed like a pauper. It stirs Selefkidis' *amour propre* as an aspiring Greek monarch to find another Greek monarch so blatantly failing to maintain "a certain dignity / at least in [his] appearance," even if the Ptolemies are now to his mind "something like servants / to the Romans." He goes so far as to offer Ptolemy VI a display of robes, jewels, and horses so that he can present himself "as he should, / as an Alexandrian Greek monarch." But Ptolemy proves himself an Alexandrian Greek monarch in a more basic mode—a Cavafian mode—by turning down all these luxuries in order to assume the appropriate costume and bearing for the performance that lies ahead: that of presenting himself to the Senate as "a poor, ill-fated creature" so that his plea for aid in recovering the throne from his brother will be more effective. And history tells us that it ultimately was: certainly a more efficacious bit of theatre than the show that Antony and Cleopatra staged in the Alexandrian Gymnasium 130 years later. Cavafy's myth teaches that shrewdness in confronting the powers that be is proper Alexandrian wit; but hunger for power, treading on corpses, and phony empire building clearly lead to hubris.

The poems of this period that describe specific, identifiable moments in the history of Alexandria—whether during the Ptolemaic or post-Ptolemaic centuries—are as subject to the poet's creative manipulation as are those poems in which the historical context is left deliberately vague and undated. And they are as crucial in shaping the architecture of his mythical city. This is not to suggest that Cavafy distorts history at will for poetic purposes. It would be difficult to catch him out on the factual background of the material he uses or even to challenge his interpretation of this material in the light of the historical evidence that was available to him. His mode is not to alter the essential substance of what his local history provides him or to offer entirely arbitrary interpretations, but rather to select and highlight that which is both true to his view of the historical moment and relevant to the particular ideology, the particular way of life, he wishes to project, a process that often leads him into the byways of history (as in "Kaisarion" and "From the School of the Renowned Philosopher"). His mode is also to search behind the obvious, established implications of familiar history for those sometimes hidden meanings and attitudes that are most congenial to his myth (as in the various poems of the Antony-Cleopatra cycle). The influence of these specific historical poems on the portrait of "our life" that emerges from the more general undated poems about Cavafy's ancient city (for example, the epitaph group) gives the portrait both a larger element of historical veracity and a broader point of view, one that allows additional political and philosophical perspectives. The typical citizen of Cavafy's mythical city—his generic hero, if you will—is, in these poems, something more than the proud, beautiful, hedonistic, artistic, Philhellenic, occasionally learned, occasionally intolerant and cynical protagonist that we saw in the epitaphs and related poems; though he continues to manifest many of these attributes, he also reveals political shrewdness, a capacity to see things for what they are, an aptitude for play-acting, a love of spectacle, some cunning in the face of those who control his destiny, some insight into the arrogant ways of men and gods, and just possibly some understanding of Cavafian hubris and the various avenues to disaster, earned and unearned.[12]

Cavafy's selective re-creation of history (both specifically dated and undated), his discovery of hidden metaphoric meanings in familiar historical moments, and his conscious attempt to embody a particular way of life in imaginary characters wearing the trappings of history, are what permit us to speak of his major preoccupation in this decade as the dramatization of a myth. The literal history of Alexandria is neither so selectively organized, nor so metaphoric, nor so populated with Alexandrians of a Cavafian kind—and the historical record of it shouldn't be. The historian's function is to create an image of what actually happened to a given people in a given place. The poet's purpose, when he makes use of history, is to discover the poetic—the metaphoric, the representative, the perennial—significance of what happened, not necessarily in the way it actually happened but in the way it ought to have happened if its underlying poetic significance were to be revealed. If the poet is also a Cavafy—or an Eliot or a Pound or a Seferis—he will organize the metaphors he has gathered from history so as to offer his readers a consistent, general structure for his meanings, a poetic structure equivalent to the setting, characters, and plot of fiction, and this structure is what can best be called his myth. In this period Cavafy's myth brings coherence to the particular way of life represented by his fictional-historical characters, the life contained in the constantly repeated if always expanding metaphor, "Alexandria" or "Alexandrian."

It is a very special life, a charmed life, for all the poet's hinting at its dark side, its courting of hubris and other excesses that signal an ultimate doom; and that which is special in it—another kind of "mythic" element, if you will—comes across clearly when we view it beside its contemporary equivalent, a juxtaposition of past and present that the poet intended to be continuous, as we saw in the third chapter. The comparison of Cavafy's ancient epitaphs and the modern epitaph "Days of 1909, '10, and '11" highlighted some of the differences between the two planes of Cavafy's parallel between past and present. Additional differences appear when we bring the more specifically historical poems into the comparison. In summary we can say that political shrewdness, play-acting beyond the personal level, a passing knowledge of gods, and a commitment to see things for what they are, along with creativity, learning, elegance, luxury, a love of art, spectacle, decoration, and things Greek—all those things that contribute to a sense of the good life in Cavafy's mythical city—are almost totally missing from his image of contemporary Alexandria. Nor is the artistic bias as alive in contemporary Alexandria; although we do find a young poet (actually a "practitioner of the art of words") and an amateur painter among its citizens, they are insignificant, it seems, beside Raphael and Ammonis, and in any case the principal continuing manifestation of the bias is in the poet's characterization of himself and his poetic commitment as these emerge from subjective poems such as "I've Looked So Much . . . ," "Understanding," and "I've Brought to Art." What remains to suggest a substantial affinity between the two planes is in the hedonistic bias: the sense that a worship of pleasure among the young and the beautiful has been endemic to Alexandria through the ages, as has the danger of excess that attends an "over-riding devotion / to perfectly shaped, corruptible white limbs," as Ianthis put it in "Of the Jews (A.D. 50)." If the poet's primary motive in presenting his two-plane myth was to illustrate the disparity between the relatively sterile, impoverished, one-sided life of the present and the relatively fulfilling, certainly more complex and subtle life of the great Alexandrian past, then a secondary motive—the other side of the coin—was to illustrate how much Alexandria goes on being Alexandria still for those who worship the same god that Lagides, Antony, Ianthis, Myrtias, and Ammonis worshiped during the ten centuries of Cavafy's mythical city that their lives serve to define.

chapter five

The World of Hellenism

The extension of Cavafy's myth, from a specifically Alexandrian microcosm to the macrocosm one might designate as the world of Hellenism, began during the years when the poet first started shaping his Alexandrian image and continued until the very end of his career; but Cavafy seems to have deliberately reserved the major expense of talent for this concern until after his mythical city had been fully delineated. From 1911 through 1917, his richest "Alexandrian" years, Cavafy published some ten poems having to do with the ancient world beyond his home city, but only six of these contributed substantially to the extension of his myth. From 1918 through 1928, on the other hand, he published thirty-four poems that explore the world of Hellenism beyond Alexandria and that extend his myth significantly; and, during the same period, we find only fourteen poems specifically about ancient Alexandria, the majority of these appearing before 1922. We can conclude, therefore, that once Cavafy had established his essential myth, his preoccupation began to shift to the more comprehensive Hellenic world of which Alexandria remained the focal center, and this larger world then became his principal concern, remaining so throughout the late years of his maturity.

The six poems of the 1911-17 period that extend Cavafy's myth beyond Alexandria provide an early gloss on the poet's intention in broadening the range of his "historical" survey, especially when they are supplemented by two unpublished poems of the same period. These eight poems also give us an outline of the new boundaries that came to define the poet's central preoccupation in his later years. The first to appear, "Philhellene" (1912)[1], introduces the concept "Hellenism" and establishes some of its Cavafian connotations, just as "The God Abandons Antony" established, in the previous year, the basic connotations of the concept "Alexandria." In "Philhellene," Hellenism is presented as the single index to civilization among barbarians aspiring to rise above their appointed role in history. Progress for the barbarian is equated with his being Hellenized; and to be a lover of things Greek, or to pretend to be a lover of things Greek, demonstrates a recognition of the life that really counts, however far out of reach it may remain.

The "philhellenic" coinage ordered by the barbarian king of this poem reflects some of the specific values represented by the term Hellenism in the Eastern provinces of Cavafy's poetry: skillful engraving, an elegant inscription in the Greek language, the choice of a young, good-looking discus-thrower as "something very special," and the apparent regard for Hellenism—all values that remind us of elements in Cavafy's Alexandrian image. On one level, the puppet king of this unnamed Eastern territory "behind Zagros, out beyond Phraata"—so fearful of possibly offending the Roman proconsul in the area—has only a ludicrous sense of what it means to be truly Hellenized: "sophists do come to us from Syria, / and versifiers, and other triflers of that kind. / So we're not, I think, un-Hellenized." At the same time he reveals, despite himself, a Cavafian propensity for the Hellenic way of life, with its emphasis on artistic skill, elegance, the young and beautiful, and the Greek language. And he also reveals a touch of Alexandrian snobbery in his dismissal of "that broad kind" of diadem "the Parthians wear" and in his wonderfully self-condemning reference to the imitative philhellenism of "so many others more barbarian than ourselves." For all his affectation, his phoniness, his barbarian pretension, he shows himself to be at least a parody of the Hellene he aspires to be, not unlike the unfortunate "Prince from Western Libya." And though he lacks a proper degree of self-awareness—the least forgivable sin in Cavafy's mythical world—his eyes seem at least partly open to the provincial reality of the un-Hellenized territory "out beyond Phraata" that he is doomed to live in.[2]

"Philhellene" outlines some of the new dimensions of Cavafy's Hellenism by showing us a remote aspiration rather than a realization, an image of what largely isn't there rather than of what prevails—in this sense a definition almost by default—and it does so by taking us to the farthest periphery of the Hellenistic world that the poet had begun to create in these years, an isolated region in the barbarian East beyond Media, where the occasional visit of a sophist or versifier from Syria is all that is known of actual Hellenism. "Herodis Attikos," published two months after "Philhellene," returns us to the center of the Hellenized world, identified in the poem by three of the cities that inter-

ested Cavafy most after Alexandria: Antioch, Beirut, and Selefkia, all belonging to the region that the poet called Syria. The
poem's speaker is at the opposite extreme from the barbarian
king of the earlier poem; he is a cosmopolitan Hellene who
shares a sense of community with all other Greeks devoted to his
kind of life, those "young men now in Alexandria, / in Antioch
or Beirut," being "trained by Hellenism as its future orators,"
who meet "at choice banquets / where the talk is sometimes
about fine sophistry, / sometimes about their exquisite love
affairs." When the speaker identifies Alexander of Selefkia as
"one of our better sophists," the "our" refers not only to those
Greeks living in Syria but to all Hellenes who share the same preoccupations and attitudes (the speaker's home city remains, in
any case, unspecified). We have seen that these trainees of Hellenism, these apprentice orators, demonstrate a proper Alexandrian balance between love and learning; but the attitude that
dominates the poem is the sense of self they reveal in recognizing
and celebrating the great orator Herodis Attikos, the master
whose fortune is made a metaphor for both their aspiration and
their superiority as Hellenes:

[They] suddenly find their attention wandering and fall silent.
Their glasses untouched,
they think about Herodis' good fortune—
what other sophist has been given this kind of honor?
Whatever his wish, whatever he does,
the Greeks (the Greeks!) follow him,
not to criticize or debate,
not even to choose any longer,
only to follow.

If the measure of Herodis' glory is his being followed at his
will by the Greeks, the implication regarding the Greeks is that
they do not follow easily nor give out glory to any but those
meeting the most exacting standards, an implication reinforced
by the speaker's rhetorical exclamation "(the Greeks!)." Their
normal mode is to criticize, to debate, to exercise their will as
they choose to, in short, the Alexandrian mode. The poem thus
celebrates not only the superiority of Herodis Attikos as master

orator and hero of Hellenism's trainees, but also the superiority of those who have chosen to follow him with praise.

The Greeks of the speaker's exclamation are specifically Athenians, the only direct reference to the Greeks of Athens in Cavafy's mature work. The speaker does not appear to be exploiting any clear distinction in attitude between these Athenian Hellenes, offering their unreserved homage to Romanized Herodis, and the awed Hellenes in training outside Greece proper, especially since he describes the normal stance of the Athenians in terms so reminiscent of Cavafy's Alexandrians. At the same time, the posture in the second stanza of the poem is that of Greeks in Alexandria, Antioch, and Beirut turning their reverent attention toward the city where the main action seems to be taking place, where the life of the mind represented by Herodis and "the Greeks" seems to find its noblest embodiment.

The subtle distinction between mainland Greeks and those Hellenes who in large part constitute the citizenry of Cavafy's mythic world—a theme merely hinted at here—becomes the central concern in "Returning from Greece," a poem written two years after "Herodis Attikos" appeared but never published during the poet's lifetime. The speaker in this poem, a Greek philosopher who has been visiting the mainland and is now returning to "the waters of our own countries—Cyprus, Syria, Egypt," reveals himself from the start to be a model Hellene in the Cavafian mode by insisting on seeing himself for what he is. He tells his companion, a philosopher and Hellene of the same persuasion:

> . . . Ask your heart:
> didn't you feel happier
> the farther we got from Greece?
> What's the point of fooling ourselves?
> That wouldn't be properly Greek, would it?
>
> It's time we admitted the truth:
> we're Greeks also—what else are we?—
> but with Asiatic tastes and feelings,
> tastes and feelings
> sometimes alien to Hellenism.

The virtue of seeing yourself for what you are becomes two-fold for these non-mainland Hellenes: they thus avoid any trace of the comic affectation, the servility, of "some of our petty kings . . . / who through their showy Hellenified exteriors / (Macedonian exteriors, naturally) / let a bit of Arabia peep out now and then, / a bit of Media they can't keep back," then find themselves ludicrously trying to cover up the provincialism they have shown; and, more importantly, these self-aware Hellenes can avoid feeling ashamed of "the Syrian and Egyptian blood in our veins"—in fact they can now "honor it, delight in it."

This poem brings into clear contrast the three faces of Hellenism that earlier poems have sketched: that of the mainland Greeks (Macedonians here and Athenians in "Herodis Attikos"), the critical, demanding standard-bearers of Hellenism and the objects of emulation among those aspiring to the name Hellene; that of the diaspora Greeks of Cavafy's ancient world (Egypt and Syria first of all) who bring to Hellenism "Asiatic tastes and feelings," which are sometimes "alien" to Hellenism but which in right measure and combination can be the source of the particular pride, passion, and self-awareness that characterize the Hellenes of Cavafy's mythical city; and that of the provincial pretenders to Hellenism, represented by the petty kings of this poem, with their "showy Hellenified exteriors," and by the earlier "not . . . un-Hellenized" Philhellene. Of the two honest faces of Hellenism, Cavafy clearly identifies—in "Returning from Greece" and in general—more with the second than the first, as is also suggested by the view of himself that he expressed to Stratis Tsirkas: "I too am Hellenic [or "a Hellene": Ἑλληνικός]. Notice how I put it: not Greek ['Ἕλλην], nor Hellenized [or "Hellenified": 'Ἑλληνίζων], but Hellenic ['Ἑλληνικός]."[3] The terms are open to various readings, and the poet uses the word Ἑλληνικός with reference to both Greeks and Hellenes, but the distinctions his remark explores would seem to parallel the three categories we have seen in "Returning from Greece": Greeks of the mainland, Hellenes of the diaspora, and "Hellenified" or "Philhellenic" pretenders to Hellenism.

Cavafy's identification with—and consistent preference for—the second of these categories appears to support E. M. Forster's estimate of Cavafy's attitude toward Greece:

[He] was a loyal Greek, but Greece for him was not territorial. It was rather the influence that has flowed from his race this way and that through the ages, and that (since Alexander the Great) has never disdained to mix with barbarism, has indeed desired to mix; the influence that made Byzantium a secular achievement. Racial purity bored him, so did political idealism . . . . The civilization he respected was a bastardy in which the Greek strain prevailed, and into which, age after age, outsiders would push, to modify and be modified.[4]

It might be more accurate to say that the civilization he loved, and normally used, was a bastardy in which the Greek strain prevailed, but the civilization he respected—from some distance, with some coldness, like the two philosophers of the poem we have been considering—was the Hellenism of Greece proper, specifically the models provided by the mainland Greek tradition in language, literature, art, ceremony, and love, the tradition sometimes identified in Cavafy's work by the phrase "the Greek way of life." What Forster's estimate rather slights is the measure of chauvinism that a "loyal Greek" even of Cavafy's broad-minded, relatively eclectic persuasion seems inevitably to manifest through an abiding respect for this Greek tradition: what one might call the cultural, rather than political, chauvinism of Hellenes. The poem of this period that perhaps best dramatizes the "bastardy" of which Forster speaks, "In a Town of Osroini" (1917), concludes with an evocation of Plato's Charmidis, the model for that element of perfection, of pure physical beauty, still to be found in the hybrid "mixture" ($κρ\acute{α}μα$) that the poem's Remon represents:

Yesterday, around midnight, they brought us our friend Remon,
who'd been wounded in a taverna fight.
Through the windows we left wide open,
the moon cast light over his beautiful body as he lay on the bed.
We're a mixture here: Syrians, migrated Greeks, Armenians,
   Medes.
Remon is one of these too. But last night,
when the moon shone on his sensual face,
our thoughts went back to Plato's Charmidis.

If the "bastardy," the mixture, is here redeemed by the resurrection of Charmidis' ghost in the body of wounded Remon, citizen of Cavafy's outlying Eastern world,[5] in "Poseidonians" the barbarism to which Forster sees Cavafy so receptive quite overwhelms a Greek colony on the Western periphery of Hellenism, and it does so disastrously.[6] The epigraph from Athenaios tells us that the Greeks who settled in Poseidonia (the Roman Paestum) of the Tyrrhenian Gulf "became barbarized as Tyrrhenians or Romans and changed their speech and the customs of their ancestors." Yet they still clung tenaciously to one remnant of their tradition, a Greek festival that they celebrated each year, calling up from memory "their ancient names and customs"; then, "lamenting loudly to each other and weeping," they would "go away." Cavafy's poem elaborates only slightly on the epigraph in presenting the historical context and occasion; the heart of the poem is the poet's explanation of the weeping and lamentation at the conclusion of the festival:

And so their festival always had a melancholy ending
because they remembered that they too were Greeks,
they too once upon a time were citizens of Magna Graecia.
But how they'd fallen now, how they'd changed,
living and speaking like barbarians,
cut off so disastrously from the Greek way of life.

This poem offers a rather different image of Cavafy's attitude toward bastardy and barbarism than the one Forster projects; it also implies (as I have suggested elsewhere)[7] that for a Hellene to be cut off from the Greek tradition of his ancestors, from the Greek language and the Greek way of life, is a kind of fall from paradise. A corollary implication is that those who come closest to paradise on earth, closest to the region of the gods, are Hellenes of the diaspora who remain loyal disciples of Hellenism without losing "the best of all things": the particular virtue that comes with being Ἑλληνικός in the Cavafian sense. This is one of the implications that emerges from "Epitaph of Antiochos, King of Kommagini" (1923), among the poet's most generous and least ambiguous descriptions of a non-mainland Hellene. The characters of this poem (except, perhaps, the unidentified Antiochos of the title) are all imaginary, unrestricted by a particular history, circumstances that permit a relatively general reference for the sentiments expressed by "the Ephesian sophist" Kallistratos, called in on the advice of Syrian courtiers to write an epitaph for the King of Kommagini—the geographical origins of these figures representing three areas boasting diaspora Hellenes. There is no evident room for irony in what the epitaph says, and we sense much shared pride:

"People of Kommagini, let the glory of Antiochos,
the noble king, be celebrated as it deserves.
He was a provident ruler of the country.
He was just, wise, courageous.
In addition he was that best of all things, Hellenic [Ἑλληνικός]—
mankind has no quality more precious:
everything beyond that belongs to the gods."

One region that Cavafy portrays during this early period as almost a paradise on earth is the land that provided the richest soil for the Greek tradition and the Greek way of life before Athens and the mainland came to dominate the world of Hellenism: the region called Ionia in Asia Minor.[8] The beautiful lyric "Ionic" (1911) speaks of the time when the Christians (the poem's "we") came into Ionia to break the statues of the gods, to drive them out of their temples. But Greek gods are not so easily exorcised, at least not those who have once loved this divine country, still potent with the ghosts of the young and the beautiful:

That we've broken their statues,
that we've driven them out of their temples,
doesn't mean at all that the gods are dead.
O land of Ionia, they're still in love with you,
their souls still keep your memory.
When an August dawn wakes over you,
your atmosphere is potent with their life,
and sometimes a young ethereal figure,
indistinct, in rapid flight,
wings across your hills.

A related image of Ionia emerges from "Orophernis" (1916), where the protagonist—a royal drifter through the world of Hellenism, born in Cappadocia, brought up in Ionia, for a while ineffective king of Cappadocia, finally an unsuccessful plotter in Syria—ends up a forgotten figure in history except for a sensuous representation of him on a four drachma coin that conveys something of the one distinguished period during his undistinguished career:

Oh those exquisite Ionian nights
when fearlessly, and entirely in a Greek way,
he came to know sensual pleasure totally.
In his heart, Asiatic always,
but in manners and language, a Greek;
with his turquoise jewelry, his Greek clothes,
his body perfumed with oil of jasmine,
he was the most handsome, the most perfect
of Ionia's handsome young men.

This passage reflects the same erotic emphasis that colored Cavafy's image of ancient Alexandria, except that here the poet
explicitly identifies the "Greek way" with an ultimate knowledge
of sensual pleasure (ἐγνώρισε πλήρη τὴν ἡδονή); and it becomes
clear that though Orophernis will remain Asiatic always in his
heart, what the Hellenism of Ionia has supplied in manners,
dress, language, and erotic technique will shape his days hence-
forth and provide the essential tone of his presence: that "sensuous image of an Ionian boy" which the four drachma coin, his
only epitaph, successfully captures and commemorates.

"One of Their Gods" (1917) is the other poem of this period
that gives us a clear image of the Cavafian figure who is devoted
to—not to say overwhelmed by—"the Hellenic kind of pleasure"
(as Cavafy puts it in the "unpublished" poem "The Photograph").[9] The setting of this undated "historical" poem is one of
a number of Hellenistic cities called Selefkia (again, the lack of
specificity in time and place permits a broadened image).[10] As in
"Ionic" the action focuses on the appearance of a god in mortal
territory, and his presence there suggests the quality of life—
specifically of erotic life—that this Cavafian city provides: entertainment attractive enough to bring one of "Them" down into
the streets of Selefkia "from the August Celestial Mansions." The
visit of a god obviously pays tribute to the "suspicious pleasure"
to be found in the quarter of the city "that lives / only at night,
with orgies and debauchery, / with every kind of intoxication
and desire," and the fact that the citizens watching the god moving toward that quarter wonder at first if he is "a Greek from
Syria, or a stranger" implies the godlike attributes they take for
granted in a Hellene arriving to share the life of pleasure provided by their city. The description of the god—"tall, extremely
handsome, . . / his hair black and perfumed"—reminds us of

"perfumed . . . most handsome, . . most perfect" Orophernis. But this god is real; he moves with "the joy of being immortal in his eyes," and that gives him a particular virtue that no other hedonist of Cavafy's Hellenistic world—Alexandrian, Ionian, Selefkian, or otherwise—can boast: that of being impervious to the mortal consequences of the earthly pleasure dome he has come down to explore. Yet for all his divinity, the fact is that when the entertainment sought is sensual, this god chooses to leave those "August Celestial Mansions" for Cavafy's city to become, for the moment, "one of them" in lower case. The poet moves cunningly—by way of conceit—in making his point: from the casual lower-case figure of the opening line, to the mysterious, extremely handsome apparition walking through the city "like a young man," to the godlike Greek from Syria or elsewhere, and finally, for "some who looked more carefully," to one of "Them" with a capital "T," literal god of this fiction, bringing the tribute of his presence to the Hellenistic city of sensual delight that the poet has created.

The poems of the 1911-17 period having to do with the broader world of Hellenism do not offer an image of the good life as detailed or as complex as the image that emerges from Cavafy's treatment of ancient Alexandria during the same period, but they do demonstrate that the poet believed this life had taken root to some extent in other regions of the territory that Alexander conquered: regions still "Hellenic" in ways compelling enough to earn the special attention of what Greek gods remained. The ways include Cavafian elements familiar from his Alexandrian poems of this period: some love of learning (specifically sophistry), much interest in love affairs, the worship of godlike physical beauty, devotion to suspicious and other pleasures, an honest self-awareness, and a respect for things Greek. What these poems add to Cavafy's image, along with extending its boundaries, are the pride a Hellene can—even should—feel in the Asiatic or Syrian or Egyptian blood that he carries with his Hellenism, whether he remains Asiatic in his heart—always while assuming a Hellenic dress and mode of life—or whether he honors the Asiatic tastes and feelings that distinguish him from a mainland Greek; and, at the same time, the pride a diaspora Hellene can and should demonstrate toward the Greek past that helped to shape him, whether contained in the beauty he manifests within the "mixture" he has become or in the language and tradition that he loses at his peril.

It is perhaps an expanding exploration of Hellenic pride that best characterizes Cavafy's shift in primary focus, after 1917, from Alexandria to the larger world of Hellenism, specifically his less emphatic concern with dramatizing the particular pride of being Alexandrian—so basic to the poems of the 1911-17 period that establish his mythical city—and his growing concern with defining the more tenuous, more complicated, more vulnerable pride of being a Hellene outside Alexandria, in a diaspora world where continuing access to glory, luxury, learning, tradition, and all else that originally served to make Alexandria "Queen of the Greek world, / genius of all knowledge, of every art" became rather more difficult, and where the tensions involved in sustaining "the Greek way of life" were rather more severe. In any case, as the poet became, after 1917, more and more preoccupied with the world of Hellenism, it was often this kind of tension—the struggle for survival of Hellenic values in the face of historical change, or the pressures that confronted Hellenism under alien regimes—that he chose to explore and represent. Though his interest now covered broader territory, it still remained highly selective geographically and temporally. After 1917, his Hellenistic and post-Hellenistic poems concentrate heavily on Syria: Antioch first of all, Sidon and Beirut secondarily. Some fifteen poems are devoted to this region, including several that do not offer a dated historical context. We find a few poems that refer to cities in Asia Minor (Kommagini, Amisos, Tyana, Sinopi, Nicomedia); there are also two poems set in Judaea, and one each in Italy, Sicily, Libya (Kyrini), and Persia. That is all. Syria, and the city of Antioch in particular, seemed to function for the poet as new mythic country, developed in detail during these years to present a possible analogy to the poet's mythical Alexandria.[11] And only three short periods of Syrian history interested Cavafy: from the Battle of Magnesia, 190 B.C., to the reign of Alexander Valas, 150-145 B.C.; under Julian the Apostate in the middle of the fourth century A.D.;

and under Christianity, A.D. 400-450. In each of these periods Hellenism was severely tested by historical change. The two other periods of Greek history that served to focus Cavafy's broader concern during these late years were the Byzantine Empire, 1078 to 1453—an interest that held him from 1920 to 1927 —and the period 220 to 200 B.C., especially with reference to Sparta, a preoccupation during his last productive years, 1928-1931.

The several undated "historical" poems about Antioch present a general image that has strong affinities with the poet's mythical Alexandria. In "Greek from Ancient Times" (1927), we find a city that, under the right name, could represent the glory of the Ptolemies in most ways:

Antioch is proud of its magnificent buildings,
fine streets, the lovely countryside around it,
its teeming population; proud too
of its glorious kings, its artists and sages,
its very rich yet prudent merchants.
But far more than all this,
Antioch is proud to be a city
Greek from ancient times, related to Argos
through Ione, founded by Argive colonists
in honor of Inachos' daughter.

We see here many of the same attributes that made Alexandria "Queen of the Greek world": magnificent buildings, glorious kings, artists, sages, rich merchants. But in keeping with the poet's emphasis during these years, Antioch's greatest pride is of a kind peculiar to the broader world of Hellenism: the affiliation this city can boast with the most ancient Greek tradition through its founding by Argive colonists in honor of King Inachos' daughter, Io, who, according to one legend, was driven to Syria by jealous Hera after Zeus had changed Io into a heifer in an unsuccessful attempt to disguise the woman he loved from his wife. It is thus a city which can claim at least an indirect (not to say adulterous) connection with the Olympian gods themselves.

The pride revealed by the speaker in "Sophist Leaving Syria" (1926) is of a rather lower order, though again reminiscent of earlier Alexandrian poems, especially the Cavafian epitaphs that celebrate, above all else, physical beauty in the greatly loved young. Here the speaker tells an "eminent sophist" writing a book about Antioch that "it's worth your mentioning Mebis in your work" on grounds that are typically Cavafian: Mebis is "unquestionably / the best looking, the most adored young man / in all Antioch." And for proof of Mebis' distinction in this regard and of his right to a degree of permanent fame, we are told that none of the others living "his kind of life" gets paid what he gets paid: "to have Mebis / just for two or three days, they often give / as much as a hundred staters." He is, in short, the most "attractive" male prostitute in Antioch, without equal not only in that city "but in Alexandria as well, in fact in Rome even." Given the competition in those cities, his is no small claim. If the "kind of life" that Mebis lives seems rather less distinguished—even less profitable—than the "our life" that Ammonis and his fellow poets lived, or the life of Kleon-Ignatios, "famous in Alexandria / (where they're not easily dazzled) / for my marvelous houses and gardens, / my horses and chariots . . . ," there are other celebrated lives in Cavafy's Alexandria that seem sufficiently similar to preclude any grand moral distinctions; for example, there is Sakkas' pupil, who exploited "the divine gift" of his beauty in the "corrupt houses of Alexandria," and Iasis, famous for his good looks in that same discriminating city and "worn out, killed" by the excesses of "our life," with its "absolute devotion to pleasure."

The moral distinction between these various lives is at best a loose and vulnerable boundary; it seems that to be beautiful in one or the other of Cavafy's mythical cities means that your beauty is likely to be exploited in some way, on some scale, and that you will likely take advantage of your "divine gift" for whatever profit it can bring in pleasure and riches. "Morality" takes on new meanings in this context. There is little evidence, through the poet's irony or otherwise, that Mebis' life is to be considered immoral in any important sense. Morality in Cavafy's mythical world is not a matter of what his contemporary society, with "all its values wrong" (as the poet puts it in "Days of 1896"), chose to consider moral or immoral. Nor is it entirely a matter of commerce either—a matter, simply, of the price involved for pleasures rendered or enjoyed. Those who prostitute themselves on a grand scale, though perhaps earning a larger share of the good life than those who settle for something less than a hundred staters in Syria or a villa on the Nile in Egypt, are not necessarily better or worse—merely more fortunate—than those denied this possibility. The only "moral" values that appear close to absolute in Cavafy's Hellenistic world are the honesty of one's response to the emotions that the life of passion affords and the virtue of pleasure given or taken for the pure joy of it. The one poem of these years that brings Syria and Egypt (specifically Beirut and Alexandria) overtly into juxtaposition serves to illustrate the point. "In the Tavernas" (1926) shows us an Alexandrian who has come to Beirut because he didn't want to stay in Alexandria after his lover "went off with the Prefect's son to earn himself / a villa on the Nile, a mansion in the city." The Alexandrian now "wallows" in the tavernas and brothels of Beirut, living "a vile life, devoted to cheap debauchery," while his former lover presumably enjoys the fruits of his high-level prostitution back in his new Alexandrian mansion. But the self-exiled speaker has gained the moral advantage in two ways: he has done the "decent" thing by leaving the scene of his rejection, and he continues to hold the memory of having possessed his lover completely for no motive other than the passion they shared:

The one thing that saves me,
like durable beauty, like perfume
that goes on clinging to my flesh, is this: Tamides,
most exquisite of young men, was mine for two years,
mine completely and not for a house or a villa on the Nile.

If the protagonist of this poem still demonstrates, in his defeat, the Cavafian virtue of a belief in passion for passion's sake, the opportunism of his lover seems more typical of the citizenry that inhabits the poet's mythical world, whether in Alexandria, Beirut, or Antioch. This world breeds opportunism, for the pleasures it provides are expensive, and the careers available—especially the public ones—are normally ruled by cynicism, influence peddling, and corruption. Survival in this world is usually a matter of making ends meet with whatever attributes one possesses and without undue concern for moral absolutes or standard virtues. As Sakkas' pupil in "From The School of the Renowned Philosopher" best represents the Alexandrian hedonist's view of social and political virtue—those "resonant banalities" of family tradition, duty toward the country, and the like —so the protagonist of "To Have Taken the Trouble" (1930) best represents the attitude of the Antiochian hedonist toward political life in his territory. Practically broke and homeless, his money devoured by "this fatal city with its extravagant life," our Antiochian decides to enter politics, a profession for which he considers himself "completely qualified" since he possesses all the attributes an aspiring Hellene entering public affairs in Syria could hope for: youth, health, a prodigious knowledge of Greek language and literature, some idea of military matters, friends among the senior mercenaries, an acquaintance with scheming and corruption in Alexandria (which gives him "a foot in the administrative world"). He is also a realist about the career he is entering: full of smart operators out to frustrate him, full of contenders for power who are all equally idiotic. Above all, he has the invaluable attribute of being able to rationalize his lack of moral scruples:

I'll approach Zabinas first,
and if that idiot doesn't appreciate me,
I'll go to his rival, Grypos.
And if that imbecile doesn't appoint me,
I'll go straight to Hyrkanos.

One of the three will want me anyway.

And my conscience is quiet
about my not caring which one I choose:
the three of them are equally bad for Syria.

But, a ruined man, it's not my fault.
I'm only trying, poor devil, to make ends meet.
The almighty gods ought to have taken the trouble
to create a fourth, a decent man.
I would have gladly gone along with him.

Of course his political ambition is more a matter of desperate wit than substance; his real ambition, one suspects, is simply to recoup enough of his losses to be able to return in good time to the fatal, extravagant life that has done him in.

The life depicted here and in other "Syrian" poems is at least as cynical, as costly, as given to excess as that of Cavafy's mythical Alexandria; it also seems to be as seductive, and ultimately as hard to give up, for all its fatality. The parallel between the two cities comes through most clearly in the following characterization of Antioch during the fourth century A.D. as a Christian society threatened by the intolerant paganism of Julian the Apostate:

How could they ever give up
their beautiful way of life, the range
of their daily pleasures, their brilliant theatre
which consummated a union between Art
and the erotic proclivities of the flesh?

Immoral to a degree—and probably more than a degree—
they certainly were. But they had the satisfaction that their life
was the notorious life of Antioch,
delectable, in absolute good taste.

To give up all this, indeed, for what?

His hot air about the false gods,
his boring self-advertisement,
his childish fear of the theatre,
his graceless prudery, his ridiculous beard.

O certainly they preferred C,
certainly they preferred K—a hundred times over.
                    [from "Julian and the Antiochians," 1926]

There is a close parallel here with the life that Ianthis found he couldn't give up in A.D. 50: the "Hedonism and Art of Alexandria" that kept him as "their dedicated son" despite his fervent declaration that he wanted to remain forever a son of the holy Jews. In both mythical cities, the seductive life consummates a union between eros and art, a union between "immorality" and good taste or elegance. The difference is that Christianity (the "C" and "K"—Christ and Konstantios—of the concluding lines) represents the "beautiful way of life" in this poem, whereas the "elegant and severe cult of Hellenism" represented that life for Ianthis; and the challenge here, the life rejected, is a prudish, moralistic form of paganism rather than "holy" Judaism. One can conclude from this parallel that the special life of a Cavafian Hellene who worships the gods Eros and Art will remain tenaciously available throughout the centuries, whatever official name is given his religion and whatever other religions try to challenge his seductive way of life.

The challenge of Julian's apostasy—his ardent but unsuccessful attempt to reintroduce the worship of pagan gods during his three-year reign as Emperor (161-163)—offered the poet a recurring theme during this period. Cavafy wrote seven poems that treat Julian and his paganism satirically, six of these between 1923 and 1933. Though some are dramatic monologues, the tone of each makes it clear that the poet sides with the Christian speaker, and in several that are not dramatic monologues, such as "Julian Seeing Contempt" and "Julian and the Antiochians," the poet (or his persona) enters the poem to comment with overt irony about both Julian's manner and his "new religious system," which he labels at one point "ludicrous in theory and application." In a reversal of contemporary stereotypes—though with proper historical justification—Cavafy sees paganism (at least of Julian's kind) as the repository of puritanical authoritarianism, while early Christianity, though increasingly colored by piety, is sufficiently tolerant and elastic during this moment of history to permit the "notorious life . . . in absolute good taste" that the poet's mythical world celebrates. That Cavafy's attitude toward Julian is not merely an eccentric or biased distortion of history can be illustrated by Julian's decree that "all who profess to teach anything whatever must be men of upright character and must not harbor in their souls opinions irreconcilable with the spirit of the state"—that is, irreconcilable with Emperor Julian's austere paganism.[12] At the same time, there is little evidence in these Julian poems that Cavafy was responsive to the Apostate's own talent for satire (sometimes heavy-handed) and for cunning self-deprecation, especially in the work from which Cavafy draws the epigraph to "Julian and the Antiochians," the *Misopogon*. In this work, Julian defends himself against the Antiochians, and their rather intolerant treatment of him, with the kind of irony one might have expected the Alexandrian poet to find entertaining were it not directed at the notorious way of life so close to his heart—the irony, for example, of Julian's commentary on his beard:

Now as for praising myself, though I should be very glad to do so, I have no reason for that; but for criticising myself I have countless reasons, and first I will begin with my face. For though nature did not make this any too handsome or well-favored or give it the bloom of youth, I myself out of sheer perversity and ill-temper have added to it this long beard of mine, to punish it, as it would seem, for this very crime of not being handsome by nature. For the same reason I put up with the lice that scamper about in it as though it were a thicket for wild beasts. As for eating greedily or drinking with my mouth wide open, it is not in my power; for I must take care, I suppose, or before I know it I shall eat up some of my own hairs along with my crumbs of bread . . . But you, since even in your old age you emulate your own sons and daughters by your soft and delicate way of living, or perhaps by your effeminate dispositions, carefully make your chins smooth, and your manhood you barely reveal and slightly indicate by your foreheads, not by your jaws as I do.[13]

Julian did not reign long enough to influence the Antiochians in any fundamental way either by his wit or his authority. It may seem odd that a regime so ephemeral should be ridiculed in so many of Cavafy's poems, especially since Julian's apostasy was, after all, an attempt to reintroduce the worship of things Greek—gods and mortal philosophers alike. But Julian's attitude toward crucial aspects of Greek culture—his view of pleasure, beauty, art, theatre, and worldly profit—were clearly at odds with Cavafy's conception of the truly Hellenic, certainly of the quality identified by the term Ἑλληνικός, and Julian's conflict with the Antiochians provided the poet with a subtle means for dramatizing certain significant distinctions even among those devoted to things Greek.[14]

Julain was readily—perhaps too readily—defeated by the Antiochians of Cavafy's world. But those committed to Cavafy's kind of Hellenism did not always have it easy during the long spread of history that concerned the poet after 1917 (220 B.C. to A.D. 1453), and it is the moments of intense challenge or actual setback for the Greek way of life that the poet most often chose to dramatize in his historical poems of these late years, as though to prove the vitality of his kind of Hellenism by demonstrating the threats and defeats it was destined to suffer, and in some measure overcome, through the centuries. Even the poem that seems to celebrate the "great new Hellenic world" of Alexander in unreserved, entirely propitious terms, "In the Year 200 B.C.," strikes an ominous note through the speaker's excessively rhetorical stance and through the date in the title: the beginning of Rome's intervention in the world described, soon manifest in the crushing defeat of the last of the Macedonian Philips at Cynocephalae in 197 B.C., and again shortly thereafter in the defeat of Antiochus III at Magnesia in 190 B.C., marking the Roman conquest of much that the poem extolls.[15] A second poem signalling the same date, "In a Large Greek Colony, 200 B.C.," also opens ominously: "That things in the Colony aren't what they should be, / no one can doubt any longer," and the poem goes on, with quiet irony, to show that no change for the better is likely in this part of the great Hellenic world because the citizens are able to rationalize inaction with a wonderful display of clichés:

Let's not be too hasty: haste is a dangerous thing.
Untimely measures bring repentance.
Certainly, and unhappily, many things in the Colony are absurd.
But is there anything human without some fault?
And after all, you see, we do move forward.

The same sense of progress toward inevitable disaster permeates the several poems about the Hellenizing dynasties of Syria during the first half of the second century B.C. In "To Antiochos Epiphanis," the king, remembering the defeat of his father at the Battle of Magnesia and the subsequent murder of his brother, wisely refuses to be optimistic about the new prospects of the Macedonian king Perseus, who, though "back in the great fight" for the moment, is swiftly and thoroughly defeated at Pydna in 168 B.C., "as was to be expected." The implication of the phrase is that history, in the shape of Rome, has sometime since taken a course that must inevitably result in the doom of the Hellenizing dynasties of the East, a course that began with the defeat of the Macedonian Philip V in 197 B.C. and that of Antiochus the

Great seven years later (Cavafy shows Philip's cynical reaction to the fate of Antiochus in his 1915 poem "The Battle of Magnesia"). Dimitrios Sotir of Syria, whom we first encountered as a proud if less than subtle Hellene in "The Displeasure of Selefkidis" (1916), attempted to challenge the course of history midway in the second century, but with no greater success. The brief account of his effort in "Of Dimitrios Sotir (162-150 B.C.)" (1919) reveals a further stage in the disintegration of the once great and no longer so new Hellenic world of the second century B.C. It had been Dimitrios' ambition to make Syria "a powerful state again" on his return to the throne in 162 B.C., to give the lie to those in Rome who believed that the heyday of the Hellenizing dynasties was over and that "they weren't fit for anything serious, / were completely unable to rule their peoples." But to his despair and sorrow he ultimately discovers that the Romans were right: "The dynasties resulting from the Macedonian Conquest / can't be kept going any longer"; his Syria has become not the "vision of Greek cities and Greek ports" that sustained him during his exile in Rome, but the land of Alexander Valas, adventurer and pretender who finally defeated and killed Dimitrios Sotir in 150 B.C. Yet in his moment of "bleak disillusion," Dimitrios continues to demonstrate how regally Greek he himself remains: the one thing in which he can still take pride is "that even in failure / he shows the world his same indomitable courage."

Of course the Syrian cult of Hellenism, the "beautiful way of life" that made Antioch notorious, hardly vanishes with Dimitrios Sotir's undoing. In Cavafy's world, politics is one thing, pleasure another. Even under Alexander Valas we find a typical Cavafian hedonist, "the most celebrated young man in town," drinking "great wines the whole night, / lying among roses" (this in "The Favor of Alexander Valas"). And as we saw, the later history of Syria reveals the same undying commitment to a variety of daily pleasures, to the "union between Art / and the erotic proclivities of the flesh," whatever the regime, be it under the moralistic pagan Julian or the moralistic Christians who followed him. The one discernible development as Cavafy's survey of Syrian history progresses beyond Julian into its final phase in

Cavafy's Alexandria

the fifth century A.D. is the impression that the cult of hedonism and art moved underground as Christianity became more conservative and more established. Two poems focusing specifically on the beginning of the fifth century A.D., "Theatre of Sidon (A.D. 400)" (1923) and "Temethos, Antiochian, A.D. 400" (1925), suggest this development. In the former we find the "son of an honorable citizen" writing "highly audacious verses in Greek" about "a special kind of sexual pleasure . . . / that leads toward a condemned, a barren love," verses that he circulates surreptitiously so that "the gray ones who prattle about morals" —presumably the established Christians—won't come across them. The image is of a society not unlike that of Cavafy's own day, the "narrow-minded" society that "had all its values wrong," which he condemned in "Days of 1896." A related image emerges from the second poem set in A.D. 400. Here the designation "Antiochians" applies not to the free-living, hedonistic society defined in "Julian and the Antiochians," but—at least implicitly —to the "unsuspecting" gray ones who have to be deceived by those called "the initiated" in this poem, clearly a group of underground cultists out of phase with the Antiochian majority. Their deception consists of a literary stratagem that Cavafy himself has been accused of using: giving voice to a contemporary homosexual passion through the mask of a historical character playing the role of loved one. Again, the union of eros and art, so basic to the "Hellenic way of life," continues to survive in these days of A.D. 400, but not in the open, sometimes flamboyant, manner that characterized Cavafy's earlier Antioch.

If there is a remnant of flamboyance in the early fifth century, it survives in what seems a too precious, too theatrical society of aesthetes depicted in "Young Men of Sidon, A.D. 400," where "five perfumed young Sidonians" have gathered to be entertained by an actor, who "also recited a few choice epigrams" that in fact constitute a rather mixed bag: Meleager, Krinagoras, Rhianos, and Aeschylus. The perfumed literati are also entertained by a "vivacious young man, mad about literature" (φανατικὸ γιὰ γράμματα) who jumps up at one point to challenge the epitaph presumed to have been written by Aeschylus in which the tragedian ignores his accomplishments in drama and commemorates only the valor he displayed in fighting the Persians. The vivacious young man finds the "sentiments" of the epitaph "weak" (λειποψυχίες) and he exhorts the group to give "all your strength to your work, / make it your total concern . . . / even in times of stress or when you begin to decline." As George Seferis has pointed out, there is some ambiguity about the poet's point of view in this poem—some question about the degree of his identification with the strong (not to say flamboyant) sentiments expressed by the vivacious young man—but the description of the context and the participating characters suggests that Cavafy views the occasion with a certain ironic detachment.[16] Literature —and some of it minor stuff—serves the less vivacious of this company merely as entertainment; their world is far removed from the world of action—of history in the making—which gave substance to both the art and life of Aeschylus. And however much the poet may identify with his speaker on the question of poetic commitment, the occasion for challenging Aeschylus remains a bit of theatre, a display of affectation and dubious taste that reflects the divorce between literary society and the realities of history that Cavafy sees to be characteristic of a civilization during the final phase of its decline, as signalled by the date in the poem's title.

One of Cavafy's "unpublished" poems, "Simeon" (1917), further dramatizes the separation between the society of letters and the realities of the world at large during the fifth century A.D. (the action takes place about 454). Here we find a sophist and his companion Mebis discussing the reputation of an imaginary poet, one Lamon, whose new poems have just appeared in Syria. The speaker knows that "all Beirut is raving" about the new work, but he is too upset to study it in detail or to talk about "books and all these trivialities" because he has caught a brief, disturbing glimpse of the spiritual peace revealed by a group of Christians worshipping in silence at the foot of Simeon Stylites's pillar. The faith of Simeon, suffering on top of a pillar for thirty-five years while "facing God," represents the new order that will come to dominate the world of Hellenism. The speaker seems to sense the power of its influence—but only momentarily. The poem ends with his return to the trivialities he dismissed at the start as he offers his listener an unstudied but nevertheless unqualified critical judgement about the day's literary subject: "whatever the other sophists may say, / I at least recognize Lamon / as Syria's leading poet." The literary life, with its arbitrary and sometimes imaginary distinctions, goes on whatever new direction life elsewhere may be taking, whatever the historical realities outside the society of letters. One such reality, at least in Cavafy's view, is the substantial change that has occured in the character of artistic and religious persuasions since Julian's reign a hundred years earlier. To have been a Christian in Julian's day was to have been at the center of an artistic life that the poet describes as "beautiful . . . notorious . . . delectable, in absolute good taste." To be a Christian now in Syria is to worship in peace at the foot of Simeon's pillar, and to be a man of letters now is to celebrate Lamon—whoever that may be—as Syria's leading poet.

There are two areas of Greek history outside Syria that briefly interest the poet in these late years: Sparta circa 222 B.C., and the Byzantine Empire from 1078 to 1453. In both periods the state had begun to disintegrate, yet both serve Cavafy as affirmations of enduring Hellenic attitudes, in particular the unassailable pride—pride in both self and nation—of Greek kings and queens. In the poem "In Sparta" (1928), we are shown the last great monarch of this ancient and once powerful city-state, King Kleomenis, at the moment when he has given in to the demand of "upstart" Ptolemy III that Kleomenis' mother Kratisiklia be sent to Egypt as a hostage to guarantee their alliance against Macedonia and the Achaian League. Kleomenis sees the demand as "a very humiliating, indecorous thing," but it proves no great challenge to his mother's indomitable pride: she agrees to go along in good humor, "happy even that in her old age / she could be useful to Sparta still." The poem concludes with a marvelous evocation of "the Spartan spirit," a Hellenic virtue that is clearly meant to outlast any particular history:

As for the humiliation—that didn't touch her at all.
Of course an upstart like the Lagid
couldn't possibly comprehend the Spartan spirit;

so his demand couldn't in fact humiliate
a Royal Lady like herself:
mother of a Spartan king.

And in a second poem about the same historical moment,
"Come, O King of the Lacedaimonians" (1929), we see Kratisiklia giving strength to her "badly shaken" son and exercising the
one thing still in her power: the grace and courage to prevent
anyone from seeing her weeping or "behaving in any way
unworthy of Sparta" now that all else lay in the hands of the
gods—including her eventual execution at the hands of Ptolemy
IV.[17]

The Spartan spirit—or at least the element of proud self-esteem
in it—becomes an object of irony to Hellenes of the diaspora
within only a few years of Kratisiklia's regal gesture, as we shall
see in the discussion of "In the Year 200 B.C." And the spirit of
Sparta's queens does not survive undamaged into the late Byzantine period, which is shown by the poet to have produced an
ample share of arrogant, plotting, and self-serving royal ladies,
for example, Anna Komnina (1083-1146), seen by Cavafy, in the
poem bearing her name, as a "power-hungry woman" driven by
the consuming sorrow of never having managed, "with all her
dexterity," to gain the throne, "virtually snatched out of her
hands" by her brother, John II; or again, Anna of Savoy, two
centuries later, who is reviled by the dispossessed speaker of
"John Kantakuzinos Triumphs" as a farcical plotter who has
never "done any good, shown any humanity." But we still find a
touch of the old Spartan spirit in "Anna Dalassini," where the
Lady of the title is eulogized for never having uttered "those cold
words 'mine' or 'yours'," and again in "Of Colored Glass,"
where the poet discovers a proper remnant of royal Hellenic
pride in the fact that John Kantakuzinos and his wife Irini chose
to wear bits of colored glass in place of jewels during their coronation, which came at a time when "our afflicted empire was
extremely poor." The poet's comment on the occasion:

                    . . . I find
nothing humiliating or undignified
in those little pieces of colored glass.

Just the opposite: they seem
a sad protest against
the unjust misfortune of the couple being crowned,
symbols of what they deserved to have,
of what surely it was right that they should have
at their coronation—a Lord John Kantakuzinos,
a Lady Irini, daughter of Andronikos Asan.

Those who see an unrelieved cynicism, pessimism, even fatalism in Cavafy's persistent focus on moments of decline and defeat in Greek history fail to perceive how much his own pride is
linked to the destiny of the tradition he represents in his work,
how much commitment to and compassion for that tradition lie
behind the dramatization of particular moments. As we have
seen, decline and defeat often bring forth vividly in Cavafy's historical characters that element of pride in self, nation, or race
that shows best under stress. And the poet's sympathies are not
only with the suffering, often doomed, often nevertheless proud
and courageous figures he portrays, but also, most emphatically,
with the much harassed tradition their individual fates serve to
characterize. The degree of the poet's sympathy in this regard,
the quality of his shared pride and sorrow as a Greek, comes
over unambiguously in the "unpublished" poem "Theophilos
Palaiologos," which comments on the final phase of the long history that has been the subject of the poet's concern in these late
years:[18]

This is the last year, this the last
of the Greek emperors. And, alas,
how sadly those around him talk.
Kyr Theophilos Palaiologos
in his grief, in his despair, says:
"I would rather die than live."

Ah, Kyr Theophilos Palaiologos,
how much of the pathos, the yearning of our race,
how much weariness—
such exhaustion from injustice and persecution—
your six tragic words contained.

The occasion is the fall of Constantinople to the Turks in
1453, the end of the Byzantine Empire, the death of Hellenism as
the medieval world knew it—hence, presumably, the total de-

spair of Theophilos' words. Cavafy's sympathetic concern—the impulse of the second stanza—is not only for this particular moment and its tragic implications but for the fate of what he calls "our race": the sorrow and yearning, the weariness from injustice and persecution, that he feels Hellenes came to know in the late stages of their history, culminating in the desperate last days of Byzantium. The identification of the poet with the Greek race is absolute in this instance, and the sentiments this identification evokes serve as a gloss on his attitude toward the Greek experience in general. He was not only a loyal Greek, as E. M. Forster suggests, but at times an ardent Greek; and the realism, the irony, the cosmopolitan eclecticism and personal idiosyncrasy he brought to his exploration of Hellenism could not erase that deep-rooted, traditional empathy with Greek aspirations that the phrase "yearning of our race" (καϋμὸ τοῦ γένους μας) most succinctly illustrates.

As we have seen, the essential effect of Cavafy's broadened exploration from 1917 to the end of his life was to provide a representation of the Greek experience that is both more complex and more comprehensive, in its geographical and temporal dimensions, than his Alexandrian image. The Alexandrian way of life, as Cavafy saw it, remained a point of focus, a touchstone for judging the quality of experience in various periods, though the specific locale was extended to include other cities—Antioch, Selefkia, Sidon, Beirut—offering their versions of the same life, their particular contribution to the concept that the poet identified by the term "Hellenic" (as distinct from "Greek" and "Hellenized" barbarian) in his conversation with Stratis Tsirkas. But the expansion of his Alexandrian image to encompass the whole world of Hellenism permitted more than simply a larger, more complicated treatment of the same central theme: it permitted a view of history, of the historical process and its implications, across eighteen centuries, from the origins of "the great new Hellenic world" in the fourth century B.C. to the fall of Constantinople in the fifteenth century A.D. His survey of Greek history was detailed enough to illustrate a substantial definition of "the yearning of our race." And to the extent that "our race," the Greek race, became a metaphor for the human race in general, Cavafy's historical survey also implied a definition of man's predicament—his pleasure and his doom, his pride and his humiliations, his changing destiny under capricious gods—through the course of centuries. In several poems of Cavafy's last years this metaphoric extension becomes the central thematic focus. An examination of the character and quality of Cavafy's aspiration toward a more universal perspective—an aspiration that perhaps best distinguishes poetry of the first order—will conclude our review of his poetic development.

chapter six

The Universal Perspective

When Seferis remarked that Cavafy gives the impression, in the poems of his old age, that "he is constantly discovering things that are new and very valuable," and that when Cavafy died at the age of seventy, "he left us with the bitter curiosity that we feel about a man who has been lost to us in the prime of life,"[1] Seferis seems to have been voicing both a recognition of the accomplishment—the wisdom and originality—of Cavafy's late work and a certain disappointment that the Alexandrian's lifelong "work in progress" (again Seferis' phrase)[2] clearly remained unfinished at his death. Cavafy himself is reported to have implied a like sense of unfulfilled possibilities when he said, during his last days: "I still have twenty-five poems to write"[3]— that is, the equivalent of one-sixth of the oeuvre that appeared as his collected poems in 1935. The reader who has followed Cavafy's development through his mature years is likely to be haunted by those unwritten poems, especially now that his archives have revealed so much unpublished work of value, all of it dating from before 1920. It would be convenient for the argument of the present study to think of those unwritten poems as the ultimate phase of the poet's development: the representation of a metaphoric mode that would bring together, and at the same time broaden, the three aspects of Cavafy's myth in progress—the Sensual City, ancient Alexandria, and the world of Hellenism—in a detailed and coherent image of the human predicament that would be less idiosyncratic and nationalistic, that might finally transcend any specific geography and history—an image more universal than those his Alexandrian preoccupation occasioned. What we actually have in his last poems are the first sure steps of a progress in this direction without the ample spread of interrelated examples that gave the dimensions of a poetic myth to each of the three images he did fully establish.

The evidence for this final aspiration rests on a few poems only, these written during the last five years of his life. The fact that they are few and scattered suggests that the poet had barely begun to shape this late discovery of "new and very valuable" things into a coherent image, if he was indeed consciously setting a pattern for the intimations the poems offer. The intimations are there in individual poems, most of all, perhaps, in the longest of those included in the canon,[4] "Myris: Alexandria, A.D. 340," printed in 1929. The historical context is immediately familiar: ancient Alexandria during a period of conflict between competing religions, even within Christianity itself,[5] about twenty years before Julian became Emperor and began his abortive attempt to restore the worship of pagan gods (though he himself was originally a Christian). The reader's familiarity with the context is assumed in the poem's strategy. At this late point in Cavafy's work, the poet could draw with confidence on the fully constructed mythical world that his three images had created for his readers over the years. He could convey the historical moment and all it implied simply by a date in the title. And he could signal the special way of life relevant to the poem's drama merely by placing the name of his mythical city before the date. The reader has thus entered into Cavafy's myth before the monologue begins, and the poet can establish the poem's particular setting and develop its particular action with strict economy. He can also assume that at least some of his readers will bring to the poem the resources in attitude and ambiance that his myth has provided, and which can now contribute to an understanding of the drama about to unfold.

The drama begins as a typical Cavafian confrontation between conflicting ideologies. We see that the pagan speaker and his dead Christian lover, despite the difference in their religious persuasions, have shared a devotion to the same familiar Alexandrian life, with its "wonderfully indecent night-long sessions," its passion for enjoyment whatever the cost, its commitment to Greek verse, its worship of physical beauty. The dead lover, we are told, "lived exactly as we did: / more devoted to pleasure than all of us . . . ." In short, speaker and lover are both among "the initiated," presumably impervious to religious conflict or historical change, committed to the Alexandrian way of life above all else. This in itself would have been a sufficient theme at an earlier stage in the poet's development of his myth (see, for example, "Of the Jews [A.D. 50]" and "Theatre of Sidon [A.D. 400]"). But the particular setting that the poet projects here raises a larger issue. The pagan speaker is overwhelmed by the Christian aura of his lover's funeral—the talk of old women about his

Cavafy's Alexandria

friend's last act of faith, the priests with their fervent, unfamiliar orisons to Jesus—and his sense of alienation in this setting leads him to doubt the shared commitment that he had taken for granted: he recalls those occasions when his friend had remained aloof from some pagan gesture that had engaged him and his other companions.

The speaker's inner drama, focused on the tension between his faith and the competing faith of one he loves, might have been a sufficient statement for the poet in earlier years. For example, in "Kleitos' Illness," the converted Christian nanny reverts to pagan gestures in the idle hope of invoking her black demon to save the life of the dying young Christian she has loved and nurtured, and in "Priest at the Serapeion," the Christian convert, who rejects all those denying Christ, nevertheless mourns for his "kind old father, . . priest at that cursed Serapeion." In "Myris" the drama rises to a new level of implication. The conflict becomes, in the concluding stanza, a struggle between the influence of Christian ritual performed by attendant priests "praying loudly / for the young man's soul" and the influence of that lost passionate life the two lovers had shared—a struggle, if you will, between Christian mystery and worldly memory:

I noticed with how much diligence,
how much intense concern
for the forms of their religion, they were preparing
everything for the Christian funeral.
And suddenly an odd sensation took hold of me:
indefinably I felt
as if Myris were going from me;
I felt that he, a Christian, was united
with his own people and that I was becoming
a stranger, a total stranger. I even felt
a doubt come over me: that I'd been deceived by my passion
and had always been a stranger to him.
I rushed out of their horrible house,
rushed away before my memory of Myris
could be captured, could be perverted by their Christianity.

The dramatic rhythm quickens to an epiphany in this stanza: from the speaker's questioning the degree of commitment shared with his lover, to his sudden doubt about the character of the passion he has held sacred, and thence to his desperate effort of affirmation. The drama has become both larger and more intimate than in other poems treating pagan-Christian conflicts, and the evocation of history in transition has here been made a means of tragic illumination rather than an end in itself. But this larger drama is not confined to the complex human predicament that the speaker's inner struggle represents. By the end of the poem, Cavafy seems to have used the speaker's dislocation to depict an act of faith within the context of his Alexandrian ideology, one that is meant to parallel (if not counter) the mystery of Christian ritual that the speaker feels is uniting his lover Myris "with his own people" and transforming the speaker himself into a total stranger. Memory—the resource that preserves and finally re-creates the transient life of the senses that dominates Cavafy's Sensual City—becomes, in the concluding lines, the one relic of the speaker's passion that can challenge the Christian influence that is being exercised to capture (and presumably save) dead Myris's soul; and the speaker's move to free his memory from contamination by rushing out of the house becomes the one act of affirmation still possible in the face of the alien mystery surrounding him. Memory remains the only recourse—the only access to some life after death—for those committed to the Alexandrian ideology. The preservation through remembrance of that lost passionate life in its purity, untouched by doubt or alien influence, seems to be the ultimate act of faith for an Alexandrian hedonist of the Cavafian persuasion. The speaker's gesture at the end of the poem speaks for all those mythical lovers, ancient and contemporary, who turn to memory for some solace and permanence when confronted by the inevitable loss that their kind of devotion carries with it. And if we recognize that the speaker's act of faith is finally as doomed as his own life (in contrast to the expectations of those serving the rival persuasion), the act seems all the more poignant.[6]

"Myris" is perhaps unique among Cavafy's mature poems in its effective accommodation of the full resources of the poet's "mythical method," resources that were the product of his having moulded his historical insight and his erotic vision into a coherent mythology over a period of almost twenty years. The particular quality of the poem, and the vitality of the poet's method when its full capabilities were realized, become all the more manifest if one compares this poem with other late poems, which either explore an image of the dying Adonis without benefit of a clearly delineated historical context, or present a historical moment without the subtle human complexities. "Lovely White Flowers," for example, published in the same year as "Myris," offers an account of two contemporary lovers whose predicament, involving the death of one and the bereavement of the other, seems pallid, almost squalid, finally sentimentalized beside the lover's predicament in "Myris," and this because little more than material gain and transient emotion seem to be at stake in their doomed affair; certainly there is nothing like an ideology or an erotic commitment approaching mystery. Nor does their predicament reflect the pressures of historical conflict and change. In the contemporary context of this poem, without a specifically identified time or place, with very little reference outside itself, belief in the quality of passion between the lovers depends on the speaker's assertion and on the reader's indulgence, a fairly demanding requisite when the passion is shown to be sustained not by any special, shared way of life or precise set of values, but by the marketplace, where loyalties are rather casually exchanged for suits and silk handkerchiefs. And given the context, it is hard to see much more than wishful thinking in the bereaved lover's claim that his friend finally came back to him from a rival bit of erotic commerce not only for the twenty pounds he has raised but also for "their old intimacy, / their old love, for the deep feeling between them." As a consequence the bereaved lover's gesture at the funeral, however sincere, seems an act of pathos, a sentimental ritual, in contrast to the lover's convincing, tragic act of faith in "Myris":

He laid flowers on his cheap coffin,
lovely white flowers, very much in keeping
with his beauty, his twenty-two years.

The poem concludes with an image that is hardly less sentimental, hardly more satisfactory in promoting the reader's confidence in the quality of the passion represented:

When he went to the café that evening—
he happened to have some vital business there—
to the same café where they used to go together,
it was a knife in his heart,
that dead café where they used to go together.

A related weakness is evident in another late poem with a contemporary setting, "The Mirror in the Front Hall" (1930), where
the poet celebrates the "total beauty" of a young Adonis, a
tailor's assistant, who arrives at the entrance to a luxurious
house to deliver a package. He arrives without much of a past or
much of a present, without either the historical or mythical context that gives substance and complexity to other such appari-
tions—in "One of Their Gods," for example—and the poet
therefore relies on personification to raise the moment to the
level of metaphor. The tailor's assistant looks at himself in a mirror to adjust his tie, and the mirror suddenly comes to life—alas,
literally:

But the old mirror that had seen so much
in its long life—
thousands of objects, faces—
the old mirror was full of joy now,
proud to have embraced
total beauty for a few moments.

The effect is more quaint than convincing: a late exercise in the
pathetic fallacy that doesn't enhance either the underlying sentiment or the overt rhetoric ("full of joy," "proud," "total") it is
intended to justify and elevate.

The poet is more successful in a similar exercise that concludes
the last poem he printed during his lifetime, "Days of 1908"
(1932). Here the contemporary Adonis figure is again presented
without benefit of an informing historical context, but he is
given a personal history that clearly links him in the reader's
mind with the partly mythical inhabitants that have peopled
Cavafy's Sensual City these many years, and the poet discovers
an appropriate rhetorical device for conveying the sentiment
that this figure is meant to arouse. The personal history in this
instance seems about as squalid as that of the lovers in "Lovely

White Flowers," a life of poverty supported by clever small-time gambling with stupid opponents and petty borrowing in "working class places" during "horrible late nights," a life symbolized by the shabby clothes ("a terrible mess") that the figure wears, specifically the cinnamon-brown suit he never changes. The suit becomes a metaphor for the seedy circumstances that our young Adonis escapes, every now and then, by stripping for a morning swim. With the shedding of "those unworthy clothes," he has an opportunity to show what is worthy—and presumably redeeming—about him: a body that is "impeccably handsome, a miracle." The miraculous, godlike quality of this apparition is established by a more subtle use of personification than that found in "The Mirror in the Front Hall." The poet ascribes his image of undressed perfection to those summer days in the distant past that had the occasion, and the taste, to observe the image in its naked purity:

O summer days of nineteen hundred and eight,
from your view
the cinnamon-brown suit was tastefully excluded.

Your view has preserved him
as he was when he took off those unworthy clothes . . .
his hair uncombed, swept back,
his limbs a little tanned
from his morning nakedness at the baths and on the beach.

The device of personification, here free of forced rhetoric, heightens the evocation rather than sentimentalizing it, and serves to reaffirm the role of memory in preserving and transforming the ordinary, even the squalid, into an image that can claim a degree of permanence in the life of the imagination.

If several of Cavafy's late poems focusing on the contemporary Adonis figure offer more sentiment than substance and rhetoric in place of convincing poetic statement, the example of "Myris" suggests that the poet had arrived in his last years at a tragic sense of life—and the controlled expression that best evokes it—which was sufficiently profound and universal to permit him in his best moments to translate his hedonistic bias and his special view of history into poetry of the highest order. Other late poems that deal directly with a historical moment point to the same conclusion, though none relates its historical context to the complexities of a specific human predicament with the effect achieved in "Myris." What emerges from these late historical poems—implicitly, never explicitly—is a general view of the human predicament, one that transcends the particular context. The aspirations and expectations of the individual historical figures, and of the society they represent, are set against the general pattern of history, what some might call the historical process, others fate, others the work of God—or, as it actually appears in Cavafy, gods. The tragic sense of life becomes manifest in the poet's subtle implication that the success of any individual figure and any specific historical moment is in the hands of the gods and therefore subject to ultimate reversal—in fact, inevitably doomed to reversal. Wisdom resides in the recognition of this limitation on human aspirations, arrogance in valuing too highly any particular success. We have seen the same theme before in "didactic monologues" such as "The Ides of March" and "Theodotos"—but in these later poems the treatment is more subtle and more sweeping. The poet's voice is always masked, his attitude that of an unexpressed conscience, and historical movements become as much the protagonists as those who represent the movements.

It is in the light of this final development that a seemingly obscure and rather dry historical evocation, "Alexander Jannaios and Alexandra" (1929), takes on more meaning than may be apparent if it is read in isolation. The poet appears to be describing that moment in the history of the Maccabees when the revolt of the Asmonaeans against the Selefkids had realized its highest aspiration under the most ruthless of the Asmonaean kings of Judaea, Alexander Jannaios. He and his Queen Alexandra, "full of their success, thoroughly satisfied," are shown to be celebrating with every kind of pomp and circumstance what they take to be the completion of "the work begun by the great Judas Maccabaios / and his four celebrated brothers." This work, described from their perspective as "relentlessly carried on / among so many obstacles and dangers," consisted in fact of great bloodshed, including a history of judicious massacres (to use John Mavrogordato's phrase) involving both internal and external enemies, not the least of which was Alexander Jannaios' massacre of the Pharisees.[7] The historical actuality behind the pomp and circumstance reminds us of Cavafy's note on "Theodotos": "Strive to become great, but don't tread on corpses."[8] The king and his consort, in their arrogant presumption of success, casually ignore the violent history that has brought them where they are by focusing on the haughtiness of those who once ruled Judaea:

Nothing unseemly remains now.
All subservience to the haughty monarchs
of Antioch is over: clearly
King Alexander Jannaios
and his wife Queen Alexandra
are equal to the Selefkids in every way.

But the poet's irony is not confined to the fact that treading on corpses occasioned the success celebrated here; the irony is directed most of all at the hubristic assumption that the "work" of years which so thoroughly puffs up the protagonists has reached a conclusion, a brilliant ending now that the autonomy of the Asmonaean Jews in their rivalry with the Hellenizing Selefkids has been firmly established. The autonomy won after so much bloodshed (yet still characterized by its own brand of Philhellenism: "Good Jews, pure Jews, devoted Jews above all. / But as circumstances require, / also skilled in speaking Greek, / even on familiar terms with Greeks and Hellenized monarchs") in fact lasted a mere eighty years, from the rule of Simon in 142 B.C., when Judaea became a free sovereign state, to the intervention of Pompey in 63 B.C., which brought Judaea under Rome after the period of further violence and dissent that had characterized the rivalry between Alexander Jannaios' sons.[9] The fate of the "haughty" Selefkids and the even haughtier Asmonaeans was ultimately one and the same; and the brilliant conclusion celebrated in this poem was no conclusion at all, either to "unseemly" history or to the struggle for Judaean autonomy and stability. But in contrast to the poet's early didactic mode, this larger implication remains unstated in any form; it is carried entirely by the poem's tone, by its irony, which depends for its effect not only on the reader's knowledge of the historical context but also on an assumption about the poet's point of view, which in turn depends to a large degree on our awareness of the perspective that the poet has developed over the years. Without this awareness, the lines that close the poem may be read as flat repetition, when they are in fact a standard instance of irony:

The work begun by the great Judas Maccabaios
and his four celebrated brothers
has indeed been concluded brilliantly,
concluded in the most striking way.[10]

If this poem points to the capacity for hubris, for blindness, of rulers who think they can prosper by treading on corpses and can retain their prosperity through the generations, whatever the will of powers beyond their control, another historical poem published in the same year (1929), "Come, O King of the Lacedaimonians," points to the capacity for dignity, for inner greatness, of rulers who accept the limits of their power and leave both their prosperity and their future to the gods. The representation is more explicit here. Kratisiklia, mother of a Spartan king, knows the facts of history: Sparta has seen its best days, and part of the evidence of its decline is her having to leave the country in the humiliating role of hostage to "upstart" Ptolemy (as we saw in an earlier poem, "In Sparta," discussed above). But it is still within her power to walk in dignified silence before her people, and it is still within her capacity to recognize that her ultimate fate is in the hands of powers beyond hers. And "the magnificent woman" says so in as many words to her distressed son, Kleomenis:

. . . "Come, O King of the Lacedaimonians,
when we go outside
let no one see us
weeping or behaving in any way unworthy of Sparta.
At least this is still in our power;
what lies ahead is in the hands of the gods."

The unstated theme is buried in the poem's concluding line: "And she boarded the ship, going toward whatever lay 'in the hands of the gods' "—that is, her ultimate execution by "upstart" Ptolemy's successor. The implication here is that dignity and wisdom do not ensure the gods' favor; the wise and the arrogant, it seems, are both subject to the same prospects, the same fatal pattern. But it is exactly her recognition of this Cavafian reality that earns Kratisiklia the designation "magnificent." Her insistence on maintaining her dignity at the moment of her humiliating departure is almost heroic, precisely because she knows that it is the right behavior even though it cannot help her with the powers that be; this knowledge is what makes it a royal act worthy of the grand history that has now turned against her.

The theme of man's subservience to the will of the gods also has its unheroic, amusing manifestation in Cavafy's late work. We have seen (in chapter 5) that the 1930 poem "To Have Taken the Trouble" offers an image of the typical realist/cynic in Cavafy's mythical world, a character who finds the various rival leaders he contemplates serving to be "equally bad for Syria," and who therefore feels justified in approaching any one of the three indiscriminately. But what stills his conscience most of all is the ultimate realization that his choice is really in the hands of "the almighty gods," who ought to have taken the trouble to create "a fourth, a decent, man" and thus have absolved him, poor devil that he is, of the need to work with one or the other of the three idiots they did create. Such rationalization demonstrates that the other side of humility can be a cunningly amoral fatalism.

Maintaining a balance between dignity and cynicism is not easy when those who see things as they are must recognize how much man is a plaything of the gods and how easily the successes of history can be reversed, but the moral balance in Cavafy is weighted on the side of those who face their destiny with courage and wisdom rather than with arrogance or an excess of cynicism, whatever the prospects may seem to be (and they are often other than what his less perceptive characters take for granted). The poem that best represents the complexities of the poet's perspective on history is the next to last he published during his lifetime, "In the Year 200 B.C.," a work so subtle in its mode that it demands careful reading to unravel its apparent ambiguities, though part of its force lies in the residue of ambiguity it permits:

the truth of an attitude that is nevertheless open to ironic treatment. The historical context is deliberately complicated by the poem's narrative focus: a monologue by a speaker living in 200 B.C. about a period of history that began some 130 years earlier. This monologue provides a survey of historical events, and their implications, from Alexander's conquests in Persia to the "optimum moment of the decline of Hellenism" (to quote George Savidis' note in *Collected Poems*), and, by suggestion, into the history of Hellenism beyond. The speaker's attitude reflects his particular historical situation, which the title, emphasizing the date 200 B.C., identifies at the start. He begins his monologue with a bit of mild irony about the Spartans, who refused at a high point in their history to join Alexander's pan-Hellenic expedition (invoked by the opening line) for the "understandable" reason, according to the speaker, that an expedition without a Spartan king in command couldn't be taken very seriously. And as a consequence, the speaker implies, the Spartans denied themselves the glory of sharing in Alexander's great victories at Granikos, Issus, and Arbela. More important, the Spartans could neither claim credit for, nor be part of, what emerged from Alexander's conquests—and here the speaker waxes eloquent:

And from this marvelous pan-Hellenic expedition,
triumphant, brilliant in every way,
celebrated on all sides, glorified,
incomparable, we emerged:
the great new Hellenic world.

We the Alexandrians, the Antiochians,
the Selefkians, the countless
other Greeks of Egypt and Syria,
and those in Media, and Persia, and all the rest:
with our far-flung supremacy,
our flexible policy of judicious integration,
and our Common Greek Language
which we carried as far as Bactria, as far as the Indians.

Given the quality of the rhetoric here and our knowledge of the particular Hellenism that most appealed to Cavafy, it is tempting to identify the poet with his speaker in these passages extolling "the great new Hellenic world" and leave it at that (as one important critic of Cavafy does[11]); but if the weight of adjectives in the first passage, and the fulsome tone of pride in the second, do not raise suspicions of some irony on the poet's part, the historical context, underlined by the title, should. The speaker is delivering his eulogy to the new Hellenism just three years before the last of the Macedonian Philips was thoroughly routed by the Romans at Cynoscephalae and only ten years before the defeat of Antiochus III the Great at Magnesia, a defeat that established Roman supremacy over the great new world the speaker is celebrating in such unreserved—not to say grandilo-quent—terms. Cavafy knows this history even if his speaker cannot. And though the speaker is merely telling the truth as he sees it—such *were* Alexander's victories and their consequences—his vision of history is limited, of course, to the time in which he lives.

The point is reinforced by the poem's concluding line: "How can one talk about Lacedaimonians now!"[12] The line may be read simply as the speaker's final sarcastic gibe at the Spartans, who are now, in 200 B.C., no longer worth talking about for all the arrogant superiority they demonstrated in refusing to join Alexander's expedition 130 years earlier; but given the broader context of the poem, Cavafy might well answer his speaker: "How can one *not* talk about the Lacedaimonians now!" If Sparta, once great and haughty, has now fallen on evil days, what is likely to befall the great new Hellenic world, now so proudly—and with this last sarcastic thrust, so haughtily—extolled? The history that followed hard on the speaker's heels provides the final comment. And with this silent comment, the poem raises Cavafy's perspective above the speaker's particular bias—one the poet himself has shared in earlier poems. The per-spective is that of the poet-historian who sees a more universal, and necessarily tragic, pattern behind even those periods of his-torical greatness that best manifest the cultural and political values he believes in: the far-flung supremacy of Hellenism, with its flexible policy of judicious integration and its common Greek language. Yet a residue of the truth expressed by the speaker sur-vives the poet's subtle irony about the speaker's attitude. If the supremacy of the new Hellenism was ultimately doomed, as was the Spartan supremacy that preceded it and the Roman suprem-acy that followed, and if the haughtiness of those on top for the moment indicates a blindness to the underlying pattern that this historical rhythm illustrates, the legacy of judicious integration and the influence of the Greek language, celebrated by this speaker, did in fact outlive his limited perspective for many generations. It is evidence of the poet's mastery in this penultimate poem that he can in effect have his cake and eat it too: he can treat an attitude with irony and nevertheless succeed in persuading the reader of the truths contained in it.

The subtlety and economy of Cavafy's late mode, in particular his ability to establish a historical context without being pedantic and to project a complex vision without being didactic —and sometimes without even speaking—illustrate some of the advantages that attended his building a myth in progress over a span of years. We come to his late poems with an established code to guide our view of his protagonists, a way of life to provide the larger context for any specific drama the poet wishes to bring before us, a series of cross-references to fill out the particular historical moment depicted, and most important of all, a pattern of attitudes to help us see the implications of his expanding perspective. As we have seen, this perspective reaches out in the late years toward a general view of the human predicament that transcends both the poet's Alexandrian ideology and his commitment to Hellenism as these were established in earlier works. The unresurrected Adonis of his Sensual City and the doomed Adonis of his Alexandrian epitaphs find a grander role in "Myris," where the fated lovers are shown to be more than sacrificial victims to the Alexandrian way of life; their predicament becomes the occasion for a tragic act of faith, an affirmation of memory as the redeeming resource of those committed to the Alexandrian ideology, even if this resource cannot bring with it the salvation in death that Christian mystery promises. And in the late historical poems we sometimes discern the poet acting as a conscience beyond the specific attitudes represented by his protagonists—some of these pro-Hellenic attitudes that he himself affirmed in earlier works—a conscience that sees any individual success and any specific historical movement subject to reversal by the gods and that shows wisdom and courage residing in the recognition of human limitations.

Some of the essential terms of this perspective were established at the very inception of the Alexandrian myth, in the poet's admonition to Antony: when the god finally abandons you, as he surely will, don't fool yourself about what is happening, face the truth of your failed mortality with courage and dignity, and make your final act a celebration of the good life you are losing. But through the course of the myth's progress, the poet's voice, rich with rhetoric and didactic authority at the beginning, becomes more and more detached, masked by a variety of dramatic personae and narrative strategies, the perspective conveyed by increasingly subtle ironies until the myth itself becomes subject to a commanding irony. The good life—the life of exquisite sensuality, refined tastes, and changing faiths— apparently thrives most either in a kind of sybaritic waste land or in a closed society of "initiated" outsiders who are more or less impervious to any ideology that challenges their absolute commitment to worldly pleasures; in either case, it is a life doomed in the end by its devotion to necessarily transient things: youth, physical beauty, passions of the moment (whether sexual, political, or religious), expensive habits, remembered sensations, artifice, theatrical performance on and off the stage, even a passing obsession with language and imaginative recreation ("Bring your drugs, Art of Poetry—/ they do relieve the pain *at least for a while"*—italics mine). The myth presents us with an image of the good life that inevitably carries within it the ripening prospect of its own death. And the poet is fully aware of this central irony; it colors his representation of the Alexandrian world throughout the canon, from "Dangerous Thoughts," through the Alexandrian epitaphs, to "Myris." Yet within Cavafy's perspective, within the world he sees, there appears to be no other life more worthy of celebration, however qualified the celebration may be. The element of ambivalence in the poet's attitude toward the mythical Alexandria he created seems, again, not the product so much of moral judgment as of tragic recognition: the good life—good as long as it lasts, anyway—is a doomed life like any other in this world; that is the nature of things, and it must be recognized. But the honest and honorable stance before such knowledge is not to reject Alexandria or the memory of the transient life it gave, but to celebrate it still for the passions it held, even as one sees the death it bears, whether

The Universal Perspective   149

the hour of recognition be Antony's at the myth's beginning or the lover's in "Myris" as the myth nears its end.

If Cavafy's universal perspective outside his myth depended on a certain detached irony—too detached, perhaps, for those with a less worldly and less tragic view of life—the detachment was not cold. The poet's sympathy, though rarely stated, clearly goes out to those who are the trapped victims of the ironies he understands and dramatizes, especially those doomed souls with the courage to see themselves and their tragic circumstances for what they are. His mockery of self-delusion, in particular among the powerful, and his sympathy for those who face their predicament without illusions are among the qualities that make him seem so thoroughly contemporary. As ironist and realist, as champion of the outsider in a society that has "all its values wrong," he speaks to the prevailing mood of our times. And his myth, in both its ancient and modern configurations, projects a vision out of the past that is readily translatable into the language of contemporary experience, whether we focus on the broken images of his waste land or on the commitment to hedonism and honest self-awareness that animated the special way of life at the myth's center. Cavafy's Alexandria, and the world of Hellenism that encircled it, so anticipated the prevailing aura of today that they now constitute a metaphor for it, in particular for the ironic scepticism about the games of nations and parties played so ruthlessly by the mighty and the not-so-mighty in recent decades, and, perhaps more significantly, for the tensions that have grown out of the shift, earlier in this century, from a faith in traditional ideologies to a faith in the self (whether conceived in Freudian or existential terms), a shift that meant to some personal liberation from outmoded taboos and to others free rein for often godless, decadent obsessions. His myth offers a model for both these perspectives, with his own perspective— the more universal perspective that has been our subject here— accommodating these while remaining, rather godlike, outside his creation, on a level where judgment can be suspended and mercy granted, though not to the viciously power-hungry, nor the puritanically arrogant, nor the blindly self-deceived.

The emergence of Cavafy's universal perspective was made

possible by the unique mode of his mature poems: by his progressive shaping of what became a largely self-contained world, with its particular system of values and its particular ordering of history, a world constructed out of a series of small dramas that, by association and growing implication, came to provide both their own composite statement and a context broad enough, objective enough, for the more universal dramas of his last poems. After 1910 the poems build on each other so as to create the general metaphor we have seen, and they do so in a way that also permits the poet's final, more or less detached, illuminations. Though the progress of the Alexandrian myth may not have been plotted with total consciousness and deliberateness by the poet (it is unlikely that any poet is ever quite as consciously programmatic as his critics make him out to be), the truth is that each individual moment on Cavafy's stage during the late years plays itself out in the reader's mind against the mythology that earlier poems have helped to create.[13] And it is this interplay between the specific moment and the general pattern that gave Cavafy occasion to demonstrate the full powers of his imagination and intellect, the full depth of his insight into the human predicament.

Cavafy's achievement is unique in modern Greek letters, and his high standing in his own country has become increasingly secure, though full recognition came slowly, and only after his death. He has yet to find his just place in relation to the more established and influential writers outside Greece who were his contemporaries and near-contemporaries. The mythical world that he built after 1910 can be seen as equivalent in its effect to the imaginative worlds fashioned by the best novelists in this century—Proust, Joyce, Faulkner, for example—and it is clearly parallel to the enterprise of those important twentieth-century poets who practiced what Eliot called "the mythical method": Yeats, Pound, Eliot himself. But, along with Yeats, Cavafy began his myth in progress earlier than the writers Eliot had in mind in his 1923 review of *Ulysses*, and Cavafy did so without benefit of Yeats's influence. The dimensions of the Alexandrian's myth may seem smaller than those of other major writers in this century, a creation drawing on fewer and shorter individual works, yet, as Eliot points out in another context (quoted by Robert Liddell in his biography),[14] "a work which consists of a number of short poems, even of poems which, taken individually, may appear rather slight, may, if it has a unity of underlying pattern, be the equivalent of a first-rate long poem in establishing an author's claim to be a 'major' poet." Cavafy's work after 1910 has this "unity of underlying pattern," and this unity is "his grace," as Seferis saw.[15] In exploring the pattern's development and its value in providing access to the Alexandrian's unique mode and perspective, I hope I have confirmed that the grace given Cavafy was sufficient to ensure his place as a major poet of the twentieth century.

Appendixes
Bibliographical Note
Notes
Indexes

Appendix: Chronological Tables

The tables in the appendixes are arranged to illustrate the two chronologies (composition and publication) and the geographical orientation of poems discussed or referred to in this book (see p. 167). The titles of a few poems not discussed here but nevertheless appropriate to a given chapter heading or category are also included (in brackets when the relevance is tenuous). The dates given in these tables are based on information provided by George Savidis in his notes to *C. P. Cavafy: Collected Poems*, notes that draw upon, and sometimes revise, the data contained in the tables that first appeared in his *C. P. Cavafy: Unpublished Poems, 1882-1923*. When a question mark follows a date, it indicates that the information available is not sufficient to establish the date firmly. Brackets around a title are also used to designate a secondary reference to a poem that receives primary consideration in another chapter and that therefore reappears under another heading.

The "Chronology of Composition" offers dates of the first drafts of poems through 1925, when the poet's catalogue of his work ends (in some instances poems underwent further revision before ultimate publication; see the notes to *Collected Poems* for the dates of these revisions). The dates given under the "Chronology of Publication" refer to the first printing of a poem, whether privately by the poet or in a periodical (a distinction indicated in Savidis' notes). The poems discussed in the sixth chapter of this book, "The Universal Perspective," are identified by an asterisk in this second chronology.

Chronology of Composition

First Draft	The Metaphoric City	The Sensual City	Mythical Alexandria	The World of Hellenism
1884?	"Elegy of the Flowers"			
1885		"When, my Friends, I was in Love"		
1892	"Hours of Melancholy"			
1892	"Timolaos the Syracusan"			
1892?				"A Great Procession of Priests and Laymen"
1892		"Blue Eyes"		
1893	"Voice from the Sea"			
1893	"Good and Bad Weather"			
1893		"Horace in Athens"		
1893				"The Footsteps"
1893	"Candles"			
1894 ?	"Ithaka"			
1894	"The Pawn"			
1894	"The City"			
1894		"An Old Man"		
1895		"Chandelier"		
1895				"Before the Statue of Endymion"
1895	"To the Moon"			
1896		"Salome"		
1896			"The Glory of the Ptolemies"	
1896	"Walls"			
1896 ?		"A Love"		
1896 ?				"Ionic"
1896				"Julian at the Mysteries"
1897	"The Windows"			
1897		"Bouquets"		
1897			"If Actually Dead"	
1898	"Monotony"			
1898				"That's the Man"
1898	"Waiting for the Barbarians"			
1899		["One of Their Gods"]		"One of Their Gods"

First Draft	The Metaphoric City	The Sensual City	Mythical Alexandria	The World of Hellenism
1900	"When the Watch-man saw the Light"			
1900	["Herodis Attikos"]			"Herodis Attikos"
1900	"Trojans"			
1901	["Thermopylae"]			
1903	"Artificial Flowers"			
1903 ?				"Theophilos Palaiologos"
1903		"Growing in Spirit"		
1903				"Craftsman of Wine Bowls"
1903		"September, 1903"		
1903		"December, 1903"		
1904		"January, 1904"		
1904				"Orophernis"
1904		"On the Stairs"		
1904		"At the Theatre"		
1904		"Come Back"		
1904				"Dimaratos"
1905				"Manuel Komninos"
1905		"I Went"		
1905				"Ionic"
1905	"The Satrapy"			
1905		"He Swears"		
1906	["The Ides of March"]			"The Ides of March"
1906	["Philhellene"]			"Philhellene"
1906				"Poseidonians"
1907			"Antony's Ending"	
1907		"One Night"		
1907		"The Window of the Tobacco Shop"		
1908		"Hidden Things"		
1909		"Days of 1903"		
1910				"The Displeasure of Selefkidis"
1910	["The God Abandons Antony"]		"The God Abandons Antony"	
1910 ?			"Theodotos"	
1911				"Tomb of the Grammarian Lysias"
1911		"On Hearing of Love"		

Chronology of Composition (cont.)

Appendix: Chronological Tables

First Draft	The Metaphoric City	The Sensual City	Mythical Alexandria	The World of Hellenism
1911 ?			"Dangerous Thoughts"	
1911		"I've Looked So Much . . ."		
1911 ?				"To Antiochus Epiphanis"
1911		"Very Seldom"		
1912			"Tomb of Evrion"	
1912			"Alexandrian Kings"	
1912			"Of the Jews"	
1913		"The Photograph"		
1913		"When They Come Alive"		
1913		"In the Street"		
1913		"To Sensual Pleasure"		
1913				"The Battle of Magnesia"
1913?				"Kimon, Son of Learchos, 22, Student of Greek Literature (in Kyrini)"
1914		"Passing Through"		
1914		"Long Ago"		
1914				"Returning from Greece"
1914		"Pictured"		
1914			"Exiles"	
1914			"Kaisarion"	
1915		"Understanding"		
1915				"Of Dimitrios Sotir (162-150 B.C.)"
1915				"Envoys from Alexandria"
1915		"Their Beginning"		
1915			"For Ammonis, Who Died at 29, in 610"	
1915		"And I Lounged and Lay on Their Beds"		
1915				"Nero's Deadline"
1915 ?		"At the Café Door"		
1915 ?		"Morning Sea"		
1916		"In the Evening"		
1916			"Tomb of Ignatios"	
1916		"Body, Remember . . ."		

Appendix: Chronological Tables

First Draft	The Metaphoric City	The Sensual City	Mythical Alexandria	The World of Hellenism
1916 ?				"In the Year 200 B.C."
1916 ?				"The Favor of Alexander Valas"
1916				"In a Town of Osroini"
1916				"Aristovoulos"
1916			"Tomb of Lanis"	
1917		"Half an Hour"		
1917		"Gray"		
1917			"In the Month of Athyr"	
1917			"Tomb of Iasis"	
1917			"In Alexandria, 31 B.C."	
1917				"Dareios"
1917				"Simeon"
1917		"Outside the House"		
1917				"Anna Komnina"
1917				"In the Harbor"
1917		"Since Nine O'Clock"		
1918		"The Next Table"		
1918		"Comes to Rest"		
1918		"The Twenty-fifth Year of His Life"		
1918 ?		[Melancholy of Jason Kleander, Poet in Kommagini, A.D. 595"]		"Melancholy of Jason Kleander, Poet in Kommagini, A.D. 595"
1918		"The Afternoon Sun"		
1918?			"Aimilianos Monai, Alexandrian, A.D. 628-655"	["Aimilianos Monai, Alexandrian, A.D. 628-655"]
1919 [1915]				"Imenos"
1919		"The Bandaged Shoulder"		
1919		"On Board Ship"		
1920				"Young Men of Sidon (A.D. 400)"
1920?		"To Call up the Shades"		

Chronology of Composition (cont.)

First Draft	The Metaphoric City	The Sensual City	Mythical Alexandria	The World of Hellenism
1921				"A Byzantine Nobleman in Exile Composing Verses"
1921?		"Days of 1908"		
1921		"I've Brought to Art"		
1921			"From the School of the Renowned Philosopher"	
1922			"Those Who Fought for the Achaian League"	
1922 ?		"In an Old Book"		
1923		"In Despair"		
1923				"Julian Seeing Contempt"
1923				"Epitaph of Antiochos, King of Kommagini"
1923				"Theatre of Sidon (A.D. 400)
1924				"Julian in Nicomedia"
1924		"Before Time Altered Them"		
1924		"He Had Planned to Read"		
1924 ?				"John Kantakuzinos Triumphs"
1925		"In the Boring Village"		
1925		"Days of 1896"		
1925				"Apollonios of Tyana in Rhodes"
1925 ?				"Temethos, Antiochian, A.D. 400"
1925 ?				"Of Colored Glass"
1925 ?				"On an Italian Shore"

Appendix: Chronological Tables

First Pub-lished	The Metaphoric City	The Sensual City	Mythical Alexandria	The World of Hellenism
1893	"Good and Bad Weather"			
1894	"Timolaos the Syracusan"			
1895	"Hours of Melan-choly"			
1895	"To the Moon"			
1896		"A Love"		
1897	"Walls"			
1897				"The Footsteps"
1897		"Horace in Athens"		
1897		"An Old Man"		
1898	"Voice from the Sea"			
1899	"Candles"			
1903	"The Windows"			
1903	["Thermopylae"]			
1904	"Waiting for the Barbarians"			
1905	"Trojans"			
1906				"King Dimitrios"
1908	"Monotony"			
1909				"That's the Man"
1910	"The City"			
1910	"The Satrapy"			
1910	["The Ides of March"]			"The Ides of March"
1911				"Sculptor of Tyana"
1911	["The God Aban-dons Antony"]		"The God Aban-dons Antony"	
1911				"Ionic"
1911			"The Glory of the Ptolemies"	
1911	"Ithaka"			
1911			"Dangerous Thoughts"	
1912	["Philhellene"]			"Philhellene"
1912	["Herodis Attikos"]			"Herodis Attikos"
1912			"Alexandrian Kings"	
1912		"Come Back"		
1913		"Very Seldom"		
1913		"I Went"		

Chronology of Publication (cont.)

First Published	The Metaphoric City	The Sensual City	Mythical Alexandria	The World of Hellenism
1914				"Tomb of the Grammarian Lysias"
1914			"Tomb of Evrion"	
1914		"Chandelier"		
1914		"Long Ago"		
1915			"Theodotos"	
1915		"At the Café Door"		
1915		"He Swears"		
1915		"One Night"		
1915		"Morning Sea"		
1915		"Pictured"		
1916				"Orophernis"
1916				"The Battle of Magnesia"
1916				"Manuel Komninos"
1916				"The Displeasure of Selefkidis"
1916		"When They Come Alive"		
1916		"In the Street"		
1916				"Before the Statue of Endymion"
1917				"In a Town of Osroini"
1917		"Passing Through"		
1917			"For Ammonis, Who Died at 29, in 610"	
1917				"One of Their Gods"
1917		"In the Evening"		
1917		"To Sensual Pleasure"		
1917		"Gray"		
1917			"Tomb of Iasis"	
1917			"In the Month of Athyr"	
1917		"I've Looked So Much . . ."		
1917			"Tomb of Ignatios"	
1917		"Days of 1903"		
1917		"The Window of the Tobacco Shop"		
1918			"Kaisarion"	
1918		"Body, Remember . . ."		

162   *Appendix: Chronological Tables*

First Published	The Metaphoric City	The Sensual City	Mythical Alexandria	The World of Hellenism
1918			"Tomb of Lanis"	
1918		"Understanding"		
1918				"Nero's Deadline"
1918				"Envoys from Alexandria"
1918				"Aristovoulos"
1918				"In the Harbor"
1918			"Aimilianos Monai, Alexandrian, A.D. 628-655"	
1918		"Since Nine O'Clock"		
1919		"Outside the House"		
1919		"The Next Table"		
1919		"The Afternoon Sun"		
1918		"Comes to Rest"		
1919			"Of the Jews (A.D. 50)"	
1919				"Imenos"
1919		"On Board Ship"		
1919				"Of Dimimitrios Sotir (162-150 B.C.)"
1920			"If Actually Dead"	
1920				"Young Men of Sidon (A.D. 400)"
1920		"To Call up the Shades"		
1920				"Dareios"
1920				"Anna Komnina"
1921				"A Byzantine Nobleman in Exile Composing Verses"
1921		"Their Beginning"		
1921				"The Favor of Alexander Valas"
1921				"Melancholoy of Jason Kleander, Poet in Kommagini, A.D. 595"
1921				"Dimaratos"

Chronology of Publication (cont.)

First Pub-lished	The Metaphoric City	The Sensual City	Mythical Alexandria	The World of Hellenism
1921		"I've Brought to Art"		
1921			"From the School of the Renowned Philosopher"	
1921				"Craftsman of Wine Bowls"
1922			"Those Who Fought for the Achaian League"	
1922				"To Antiochos Epiphanis"
1922		"In An Old Book"		
1923		"In Despair"		
1923				"Julian Seeing Contempt"
1923				"Epitaph of Antiochos, King of Kommagini"
1923				"Theatre of Sidon (A.D. 400)"
1924				"Julian in Nicomedia"
1924		"Before Time Altered Them"		
1924		"He Had Planned to Read"		
1924			"In Alexandria, 31 B.C."	
1924				"John Kantakuzinos Triumphs"
1925				"Temethos, Antiochian, A.D. 400"
1925				"Of Colored Glass"
1925		"The Twenty-fifth Year of His Life"		
1925				"On an Italian Shore"
1925		"In the Boring Village"		
1925				"Apollonios of Tyana in Rhodes"
1926			"Kleitos' Illness"	
1926				"In a Township of Asia Minor"

First Published	The Metaphoric City	The Sensual City	Mythical Alexandria	The World of Hellenism
1926			"Priest at the Sera-peion"	
1926			["In the Tavernas"]	"In the Tavernas"
1926				"A Great Procession of Priests and Laymen"
1926				"Sophist Leaving Syria"
1926				"Julian and the Antiochians"
1927				"Anna Dalassini"
1927		"Days of 1896"		
1927		"Two Young Men, 23 to 24 Years Old"		
1927				"Greek from Ancient Times"
1927		"Days of 1901"		
1928				"You Didn't Understand"
1928		"A Young Poet in His Twenty-fourth Year"		
1928				"In Sparta"
1928		"Picture of a 23-year-old Painted by his Friend of the Same Age, an Amateur"		
1928				"In a Large Greek Colony, 200 B.C."
1928			"A Prince from Western Libya"	
1928				"Kimon, Son of Learchos, 22, Student of Greek Literature (in Kyrini)"
1928				"On the March to Sinopi"
1928		"Days of 1909, '10, and '11"		
1929			*"Myris: Alexandria, A.D. 340"	

Chronology of Publication (cont.)

Appendix: Chronological Tables 165

First Published	The Metaphoric City	The Sensual City	Mythical Alexandria	The World of Hellenism
1929				*"Alexander Jannaios and Alexandra"
1929		*"Lovely White Flowers"		
1929				*"Come, O King of the Lacedaimonians"
1929		"In the Same Space"		
1930		*"The Mirror in the Front Hall"		
1930		"He Asked About the Quality"		
1930				*"To Have Taken the Trouble"
1931				"Following the Recipe of Ancient Greco-Syrian Magicians"
1931				*"In the Year 200 B.C."
1932		*"Days of 1908"		
[1935]				"On the Outskirts of Antioch"

Appendix: Principal Settings

The table of "Principal Settings" is intended to provide a comparative outline of the ancient regions and cities that preoccupied the poet at different moments in his career, though the outline does not offer a comprehensive image of the early years. The arrangement under the various headings is roughly chronological. Dates are those of first printing, except in the case of the "unpublished poems," where the date, given in brackets, is that of the first draft. The titles of poems that allude to several settings without being located specifically in one of these (e.g., "Returning from Greece") or that generalize the the setting (e.g., "In a Large Greek Colony, 200 B. C.") appear in brackets, and those poems that are located in one setting but that allude significantly to a secondary setting reappear in brackets under the appropriate secondary heading. Those poems that do not specify a particular city are listed either under the name of the country designated or under the heading "Unspecified." The heading "Mainland Greece" includes, for purposes of convenience, the neighboring islands of Ithaka and Rhodes, given in brackets.

The Ancient World of Hellenism: Principal Settings

Mainland Greece	Italy and Sicily	Egypt and Libya

Mainland Greece

ATHENS
"Horace in Athens"
(1897)
"Herodis Attikos"
(1912)
ELEUSIS
"Julian at the Mysteries"
[1896]
ARGOS
"When the Watchman
Saw the Light" [1900]
THERMOPYLAE
"Thermopylae" (1903)
MACEDONIA
"King Dimitrios" (1906)
"The Battle of Magnesia"
(1916)
[ITHAKA]
"Ithaka" (1911)
DELPHI
"Nero's Deadline" (1918)
"Envoys from Alexan-
dria" (1918)
[RHODES]
"Apollonios of Tyana in
Rhodes" (1925)
SPARTA
"In Sparta" (1928)
"Come, O King of the
Lacedaimonians"
(1929)

Italy and Sicily

ROME
"The Footsteps" (1897)
"The Ides of March"
(1910)
"Sculptor of Tyana"
(1911)
"The Displeasure of
Selefkidis" (1916)
POSEIDONIA
"Poseidonians" (1906)
SICILY
["Aimilianos Monai,
Alexandrian, A.D.
628-655" (1918)]
SYRACUSE
"Timolaos the Syracu-
san" (1894)
"Imenos" (1919)
UNSPECIFIED
"On an Italian Shore"
(1925)

Egypt and Libya

ALEXANDRIA
"Antony's Ending" [1907]
"The God Abandons
Antony" (1911)
"The Glory of the Ptole-
mies" (1911)
"Dangerous Thoughts"
(1911)
"Alexandrian Kings"
(1912)
"Tomb of Evrion" (1914)
"Exiles" [1914]
"Theodotos" (1915)
"For Ammonis, Who
Died at 29, in A.D.
610" (1917)
"Tomb of Iasis" (1917)
"In the Month of Athyr"
(1917)
"Tomb of Ignatios"
(1917)
"Kaisarion" (1918)
"Tomb of Lanis" (1918)
"Aimilianos Monai,
Alexandrian, A.D.
628-655" (1918)
"Of the Jews (A.D. 50)"
(1919)
"If Actually Dead" (1920)
"From the School of the
Renowned Philoso-
pher" (1921)
"Those Who Fought for
the Achaian League"
(1922)
"In Alexandria, 31 B.C."
(1924)
"Kleitos' Illness" (1926)
"Priest at the Serapeion"
(1926)
["In the Tavernas"
(1926)]
"A Prince from Western
Libya" (1928)
"Myris: Alexandria,
A.D. 340" (1929)
UNSPECIFIED
["Returning from Greece"
[1914]]
LIBYA
["A Prince From Western
Libya" (1928)]
"Kimon, Son of Lear-
chos, 22, Student of
Greek Literature (in
Kyrini)" (1928)

Syria, Phoenicia, Judaea	Asia Minor	Eastern Regions
ANTIOCH	TROY	SUSA
"That's the Man" (1909)	"Trojans" (1905)	"The Satrapy" (1910)
"The Favor of Alexander	TYANA	BEYOND PHRAATA
Valas" (1921)	["Sculptor of Tyana"	"Philhellene" (1912)
"Craftsman of Wine	(1911)]	OSROINI (MESOPOTA-
Bowls" (1921)	["If Actually Dead"	MIA)
"To Antiochos Epi-	(1920)]	"In a Town of Osroini"
phanis" (1922)	["Apollonios of Tyana in	(1917)
"Temethos, Antiochian,	Rhodes" (1925)]	KOMMAGINI
A.D. 400" (1925)	IONIA	"Melancholy of Jason
"A Great Procession of	"Ionic" (1911)	Kleander, Poet in
Priests and Laymen"	"Orophernis" (1916)	Kommagini, A.D. 595"
(1926)	BYZANTIUM	(1921)
"Julian and the Antio-	"Theophilos Palaiologos"	"Epitaph of Antiochos,
chians" (1926)	[1914]	King of Kommagini"
"Greek from Ancient	"Manuel Komninos"	(1923)
Times" (1927)	(1916)	PERSIA
"To Have Taken the	"Anna Komnina" (1920)	"Dimaratos" (1921)
Trouble" (1930)	"A Byzantine Nobleman	UNSPECIFIED
"On the Outskirts of	in Exile Composing	["In a Large Greek Col-
Antioch" [1932 ?]	Verses" (1921)	ony, 200 B.C." (1928)]
BEIRUT	"Julian Seeing Contempt"	["In the Year 200 B.C."
"Tomb of the Gram-	(1923)	(1931)]
marian Lysias" (1914)	["Julian in Nicomedia"	
"Simeon" [1917]	(1924)]	
"In the Tavernas" (1926)	"John Kantakuzinos	
SELEFKIA ?	Triumphs" (1924)	
"One of Their Gods"	"Of Colored Glass"	
(1917)	(1925)	
JUDAEA	"Anna Dalassini" (1927)	
"Aristovoulos" (1918)	"You Didn't Understand"	
"Alexander Jannaios and	(1928)	
Alexandra" (1929)	CAPPADOCIA	
SIDON	["Orophernis" (1916)]	
"Young Men of Sidon	MILITOS	
(A.D. 400)" (1920)	"Before the Statue of	
"Theatre of Sidon (A.D.	Endymion" (1916)	
400)" (1923)	AMISOS	
UNSPECIFIED	"Dareios" (1920)	
["Returning from Greece"	NICOMEDIA	
[1914]]	"Julian in Nicomedia"	
["The Displeasure of	(1924)	
Selefkidis" (1916)]	SINOPI	
"In the Harbor" (1918)	"On the March to Sinopi"	
"Of Dimitrios Sotir (162-	(1928)	
150 B.C.)" (1919)	UNSPECIFIED	
"Sophist Leaving Syria"	"In a Township of Asia	
(1926)	Minor" (1926)	

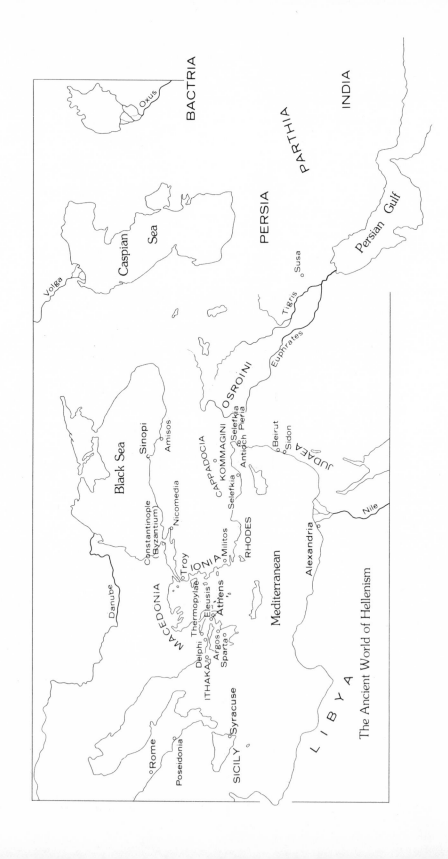

The Ancient World of Hellenism

Bibliographical Note

Principal Sources

Cavafy, C. P., *Collected Poems*, Keeley, Edmund, and Sherrard, Philip, trans., Savidis, George, ed. (Princeton University Press, Princeton, 1975; The Hogarth Press, London, 1975).

————, *Passions and Ancient Days*, Keeley, Edmund, and Savidis, George, trans. (The Dial Press, New York, 1971; The Hogarth Press, London, 1972).

Lechonitis, G., Καβαφικὰ αὐτοσχόλια [Cavafian Self-comments](Alexandria, 1942).

Liddell, Robert, *Cavafy: A Critical Biography* (Duckworth, London, 1974).

Malanos, Timos, Ὁ ποιητὴς Κ. Π. Καβάφης [The Poet C. P. Cavafy] (Difros, Athens, 1957).

Savidis, G. P., Οἱ Καβαφικές ἐκδόσεις (1891-1932) [The Editions of Cavafy (1891-1932)] (Ekdosi Tachydromou, Athens, 1966).

Savidis, G. P., ed., Κ. Π. Καβάφη: Ἀνέκδοτα Ποιήματα 1882-1923 [C. P. Cavafy: Unpublished Poems, 1882-1923] (Ikaros, Athens, 1968).

Seferis, George, *On the Greek Style: Selected Essays in Poetry and Hellenism*, Warner, Rex, and Frangopoulos, Th., trans. (Atlantic-Little, Brown; Boston, 1966; The Bodley Head, London, 1966).

Tsirkas, Stratis, Ο Καβάφης καὶ ἡ ἐποχή του [Cavafy and his Epoch] (Kedros, Athens, 1958, 1971).

Other Sources

Bevan, Edwyn, *The House of Seleucus*, vol. 2 (Edward Arnold, London, 1902).

Bien, Peter, *Constantine Cavafy* (Columbia Essays on Modern Writers, New York, 1964).

Bowra, C. M., "Constantine Cavafy and the Greek Past," in *The Creative Experiment* (Macmillan, London, 1949).

Cavafy, C. P., *The Complete Poems of Cavafy*, Dalven, Rae, trans. (Harcourt, Brace, and World, New York, 1961; The Hogarth Press, London, 1961).

———— "The Early C. P. Cavafy," Cavafy, John, trans., *St. Andrews Review* (Fall and Winter, 1974).

———— *The Poems of C. P. Cavafy*, Mavrogordato, John, trans. (The Hogarth Press, London, 1951; Grove Press, New York, 1952).

Durrell, Lawrence, *Justine* (Faber and Faber, London, 1957).

Eliot, T. S., "Ulysses, Order, and Myth," *The Dial* (November, 1923).

———— "What Is Minor Poetry?" in *On Poetry and Poets* (Farrar, Straus; New York, 1957; Faber and Faber, London, 1957).

Ellmann, Richard, *James Joyce* (Oxford, New York, 1959).

Forster, E. M., "The Complete Poems of C. P. Cavafy," in *Two Cheers for Democracy* (Edward Arnold, London, 1951).

Golffing, Francis, "The Alexandrian Mind: Notes Toward a Definition," *Partisan Review* (Winter, 1955).

Keeley, Edmund, "The Art of Poetry XIII: George Seferis," *The Paris Review*, no. 50 (Fall, 1970).

Keeley, Edmund, and Sherrard, Phillip, trans., *Six Poets of Modern Greece* (Thames and Hudson, London, 1960; Alfred A. Knopf, New York, 1961).

Malanos, Timos, Περί Καβάφη [About Cavafy] (Alexandria, 1935).

Peridis, M., Ὁ βίος καὶ τὸ ἔργο τοῦ Κωνστ. Καβάφη [The Life and Work of Const. Cavafy] (Ikaros, Athens, 1948).

Peters, F. E., *The Harvest of Hellenism* (Simon and Schuster, New York, 1970).

Sareyannis, I. A., Σχόλια στὸν Καβάφη [Commentaries on Cavafy] Zissimos Lorenzatos, ed. (Ikaros, Athens, 1964).

Savidis, G. P., Ὁ Καβάφης σχολιάζει καὶ ἀναλύει τὰ "Κεριά" [Cavafy Annotates and Analyzes "Candles"] Το Βῆμα [*To Vima*] (Athens, April 29, 1973).

_____ Πάνω νερά [Against the Current] (Hermes, Athens, 1973).

Seferis, George, Δοκιμές [Essays], 3rd ed. (Ikaros, Athens, 1974).

_____, *A Poet's Journal: Days of 1945-51*, Anagnostopoulos, Athan, trans. (Harvard University Press, Cambridge, 1974).

Sherrard, Philip, "Constantine Cavafis," in *The Marble Threshing Floor* (Vallentine, Mitchell; London, 1956).

Tsirkas, Stratis, Ὁ πολιτικός Καβάφης [The Political Cavafy] (Kedros, Athens, 1971).

Valeta, G., "Καβάφης ὁ Ἀντίοχος" [Cavafy the Antiochian], Πειραϊκά Γράμματα, vol. 3, no. 5 (May, 1943).

Vasiliev, A. A., *History of the Byzantine Empire* (University of Wisconsin Press, Madison, 1968)

Wright, Wilmer C., trans., *The Works of the Emperor Julian* (Loeb Classical Library, London-Cambridge, 1959).

Notes

Chapter 1: Introduction: The Literal City

1. See C. P. Cavafy, *Unpublished Poems, 1882-1923*, ed. George Savidis. The first English version of "Exiles" and of other "unpublished" poems discussed below appeared in *C. P. Cavafy: Passions and Ancient Days*, trans. Edmund Keeley and George Savidis. The quotations offered here, and the translations used throughout this study, are from *C. P. Cavafy: Collected Poems*, trans. Edmund Keeley and Philip Sherrard, ed. George Savidis.

2. Though the historical context cannot be established beyond doubt (the only direct clue given us by the poet is the name Basil in the penultimate line, and there are of course several Byzantine emperors of that name), a plausible theory regarding the context—pointing to Basil I as the probable reference—is offered in a note to the poem that appears in *Passions and Ancient Days*.

3. The relation between Cavafy and these writers, along with Robert Liddell and D. J. Enright, is explored in depth by Jane Pinchin in a dissertation presented at Columbia University in 1973: "It Goes On Being Alexandria Still: C. P. Cavafy and the English Alexandrians," to be published in revised form by Princeton University Press. Among recent non-English "Alexandrians," compare the impressive trilogy by Stratis Tsirkas, *Drifting Cities*.

4. From an interview with Seferis by Edmund Keeley, "The Art of Poetry XIII: George Seferis," p. 81.

5. Of his six older brothers, George and Peter John in particular: see Robert Liddell, *Cavafy: a Critical Biography*, p. 26. I am indebted to Mr. Liddell's book—the most authoritative and comprehensive biography of the poet—for much of the biographical data that follows, though not necessarily for the interpretation given this data. The English rendering of Καβάφης as "Cavafy" was traditional in the family and was used by the poet himself when signing poems and letters that he wrote in English.

6. Ibid., p. 165.

7. For an entertaining account of Cavafy's life at the office, see the comments by his former colleague, Ibrahim el Kayar, in an interview conducted by Manolis Halvatzakis ('Ο Καβάφης στήν ὑπαλληλική του ζωή [*Cavafy's Clerical Life*], Athens, 1967), excerpts from which appear in Liddell, pp. 127 ff.

8. Quoted by Liddell, p. 143.

9. For a full record of Cavafy's eccentric method of printing and distributing his poems, see George Savidis, *The Editions of Cavafy*.

10. The term has become the standard one for describing the 154 poems that appeared in the posthumous collected edition of Cavafy's poems edited by Alexander and Rika Singopoulos (Alexandria, 1935).

11. See Liddell, pp. 145 and 183-184. E. M. Forster included a sympathetic portrait of Cavafy in *Pharos and Pharillon* (1923) and intro-

duced Cavafy's work to T. E. Lawrence, Arnold Toynbee, and T. S. Eliot, among others (Eliot published a version of "Ithaka" in *Criterion*). But negotiations for an English translation of the Alexandrian's work foundered despite strong interest on the part of The Hogarth Press; according to the designated translator, George Valassopoulos, even by 1928 Cavafy did not consider his work ready for a definitive edition in Greek, and he felt a translation should not precede an edition of the original text (Liddell, p. 185).

12. Liddell, p. 167.

13. In a note found among Cavafy's papers and dated 1906 (see *Passions and Ancient Days*, p. 59, fn. 1), the poet exclaims: "By my postponing, and repostponing to publish, what a gain I have had! Think of . . . trash [written] at the age of 25, 26, 27, 28, of Byzantine poems . . . and many others which would disgrace me now . . . What wretched trash!"

14. Cavafy designated his sparingly-selected early work as "Before 1911" in the various tables of content that he printed during his mature years.

15. *On the Greek Style: Selected Essays in Poetry and Hellenism*, trans. Rex Warner and Th. Frangopoulos, p. 125.

Chapter 2: The Metaphoric City

1. The booklet, *Poems (1909-1911)*, contained fourteen poems arranged thematically rather than chronologically, with "The City" appearing ahead of "The Footsteps" and "That's the Man," both originally published a year earlier. This arrangement established an order of presentation duplicated in subsequent selections (see Savidis, *The Editions of Cavafy*, pp. 335-336, and Keeley and Savidis, trans., *Passions and Ancient Days*, p. x). The fact that Cavafy decided to make "The City" the lead poem of this arrangement as late as 1917, when he had at hand several poems of greater aesthetic merit that he might have chosen, as well as the distance in time for a proper critical perspective regarding his early work, merely underlines the emphasis he wished to give to the "city" image in presenting his poems.

2. In exploring Cavafy's development one has to deal with two chronologies, the first identifying the date a poem was originally written and the second the date Cavafy chose to print and distribute the poem, the two dates sometimes years apart (see the chronologies of composition and publication under "Chronological Tables" in the first appendix to this book). As one reviews these chronologies—a task made possible by the invaluable tables that George Savidis included in his edition of Cavafy's *Unpublished Poems, 1882-1923*—one finds evidence that the poet was interested in giving his work a particular pattern once he began to collect his poems and offer them to his private, scrupulously controlled list of readers. In addition to the implications of the thematic arrangement he gave the booklets discussed in note 1, above, it is apparent that Cavafy often issued his poems not as they first came out of his workshop but as they contributed, in due course, and

sometimes in altered form, to the imaginative world that he wished to project during his mature years. Some of the implications of the chronology of publication have been examined by critics in Greece, in particular, Timos Malanos, George Seferis, Stratis Tsirkas, and George Savidis. The latter's tables in *Unpublished Poems* correlated for the first time the dates of composition and publication for all those poems that appear in Cavafy's own precisely dated catalogues of the poetry he wrote between 1891 and 1925. As Savidis indicates in his introduction to the volume, the poet's archives reveal two catalogues, one covering the years 1891 to 1912 and the other 1891 to 1925. The second revises the first so as to delete the titles of 98 poems written between 1891 and 1912. In this study I focus during chapters 2 and 3 on the still unexplored chronology of composition, because that serves best to establish the developing pattern of the poet's preoccupations and his aesthetic progress as he worked to create both his mature voice and his central myth. In chapters 4, 5, and 6, I concentrate on the chronology of publication, because in these chapters I am more concerned with the published image of his work that Cavafy offered his select audience of readers.

3. Or even of sexual predicament, according to Timos Malanos in *The Poet C. P. Cavafy*, p. 302. Malanos's position is qualified by Stratis Tsirkas in *Cavafy and His Epoch*, pp. 248-251, in keeping with his own estimate of Cavafy's personal predicament at the time the poem was written.

4. Michalis Peridis, *The Life and Work of Const. Cavafy*, p. 312.

5. The dates offered in parenthesis after titles are those of composition.

6. *Cavafy and His Epoch*, pp. 246-247.

7. The remarks that Cavafy is presumed to have made to Politis and Lechonitis (see Tsirkas, *Cavafy and His Epoch*, p. 248) indicating that the poem applies to "What could happen in certain situations, but not that this will happen inevitably" and that it has to do "with the situation of some people, not with situations in general" strike me as unnecessarily protective. The poem speaks for itself: the situation is that of a persona (an "I" subsequently rendered as "you") who has ruined his life in a way and to a degree that preclude his escaping from what he has made of it, and the poem applies to all those who feel that they share the persona's fate or at least accept the poem's statement as valid in the terms in which it is rendered.

8. Peridis, p. 36.

9. The note, published here (and in *The Southern Review*, Winter, 1976) for the first time, was discovered by George Savidis among other notes in Cavafy's archives.

10. Except when otherwise indicated, the biographical data in this chapter is taken from Liddell, *Cavafy*.

11. See chapter 1, note 9.

12. For precise details, see Savidis, *The Editions of Cavafy*, pp. 192 ff.

13. Lechonitis, *Cavafian Self-comments*, p. 25.

14. In conversation with the writer.

15. From "In the Evening." The poem was actually written in 1916, under the working title—again to the point here—of "Alexandrinon" ("Alexandrian").

16. I have in mind Seferis's remarks on Cavafy in the interview that appeared in *The Paris Review*, no. 50, pp. 80-81. Seferis says: "Again, what I appreciate very much in Cavafy is his having started with terrifically unreal poems and then, by insistence and work, he found at last his own personal voice. He wrote very bad poems up to his thirty-fourth year. The failure of those poems cannot be translated or communicated to a foreign reader because the language of the translation is always bound to improve them . . . he was a man who starts at a certain age with all signs showing that he's unable to produce anything of importance. And then, by refusing and refusing things which are offered him, in the end he *finds*, he *sees*, as they say; he becomes certain that he's found his own expression. It's a splendid example of a man who, through his refusals, finds his way." The comment by Cavafy on his own early work is quoted in chapter 1, note 13, and more fully in *Passions and Ancient Days*, p. ix.

17. The English Romantics, and the English tradition in general, were a stronger influence on Cavafy's early development than the other sources that have traditionally influenced modern Greek poetry, e.g., French, German, and Italian literature. Cavafy lived in England between the ages of nine and sixteen. His first verse was written in English (signed "Constantine Cavafy"), and throughout his life he demonstrated his familiarity with the English literary tradition, especially the works of Shakespeare, Browning, and Oscar Wilde (see note 21). He was also fluent in French.

18. *To Vima*, Athens, April 29, 1973. In his editorial preface to the note, George Savidis suggests that it was written between 1893 (the date the poem itself was written) and 1899 (the date the first draft of it, which accompanied the note in manuscript, was published). The date can perhaps be established more precisely as between 1897 and 1899, since the note refers to "The Windows," which was written in August 1897. John Cavafy did in fact translate a large number of Cavafy's poems and collected them in two manuscripts dated 1916 and 1918, neither of which was published. For a sample of his work, and a brief commentary on it, see *St. Andrews Review*, Fall and Winter, 1974.

19. Cavafy's use of the term "allegorical" here is fairly arbitrary. He does not have in mind the traditional, technical use of the term, that is, the representation of an abstract idea through personification, much less the continuous narrative that is thought to be necessary for a sustained allegory. Cavafy's use of the term seems less precise and less specific than is customary; his so-called allegories are really extended metaphors in which not an abstraction but a predicament—a state of mind or condition of the psyche—is represented through "objects in action," for example, the objects in "Walls" and "The Windows."

20. The earliest "allegorical" poem mentioned by Cavafy in his note is "The Pawn," written in July 1894—that is, one year after "Candles"

and one month before the first draft of "The City." It is a primitive exercise in this mode and unrelated thematically to the three "suggestif" poems that interest us here.

21. The influence of Browning and the Greek anthology is explored, among other influences, in an unpublished dissertation on English and American literary sources in the work of Cavafy and Seferis that I submitted to Oxford University in 1952 (a copy is held by the Bodleian Library).

22. *House of Seleucus*, vol. 2, p. 159.

23. The designation "historical poet" was Cavafy's own, according to Lechonitis (p. 22): "I am a historical poet. I could never write a novel or a play; but I sense inside me 125 voices telling me that I could write history."

24. One should regard "Timolaos the Syracusan" (written 1892, published 1894) as a factor in this progress, because as Seferis points out (*Essays*, vol. 1, pp. 383-384), in this early and not very satisfactory poem, Cavafy first "attempts to express, awkwardly, a metropolis—a country that he is carrying inside him; the idea circles in his mind, but it hasn't yet taken on flesh; Antioch and Alexandria haven't appeared on the horizon . . . . He approaches the tone of 'we're a mixture here' [from "In a Town of Osroini"], but he hasn't found it yet." (A translation of the poem is included in Rae Dalven, trans., *The Complete Poems of Cavafy*, pp. 194-195.)

25. A third poem of this kind, "Theodotos," may have been written in the same year, because Savidis identifies the date of composition as "sometime before October 3, 1911" (see his note to the poem in *Collected Poems*). Though the poem mentions Alexandria, it does not make use of the city image in a way central to our concerns here, nor does "The Ides of March," another "didactic monologue," written in 1906 and published in 1910. The note to "Ithaka" in *Collected Poems* indicates that a first version of this poem was "probably written January 1894," that is, seven months before the first draft of "The City."

26. The source in Plutarch, where the god abandoning Antony appears as Dionysus, is *Life of Antony*, par. 75, and in Shakespeare, where the god becomes Hercules, *Antony and Cleopatra*, IV, iii.

Chapter 3: The Sensual City

1. The only exceptions that I have uncovered are two early poems, "Sham-El-Nessim," written and published in 1892, and "27 June, 1906, 2 p.m." written in 1908 but not published during Cavafy's lifetime. The former describes, rather bucolically, the Egyptian festival named in the title, and the latter focuses on a mother's reaction to the hanging, on 27 June, 1906, of an Egyptian youth condemned to death by the British, along with three of his countrymen, in reprisal for an incident in an Egyptian village during which a British officer was wounded in the head by a stone (he subsequently died of sunstroke after walking back to his barracks; see Stratis Tsirkas, *The Political Cavafy*, pp. 71 ff.).

2. The term "erotic" was one of three that Cavafy himself used in

designating the major categories of his work, the other two being "historical" and "philosophic." See chapter 4, note 3, and Savidis, *The Editions of Cavafy*, p. 209.

3. Ambiguity of gender is easily sustained in Greek because personal pronouns before a verb are not mandatory and are often omitted as a matter of course. Also, Cavafy sometimes has his persona address his subject in the second person, again permitting an ambiguity (this in his "unpublished" erotic poems as well). The progress of Cavafy's revelation in his published work was first explored by Timos Malanos in the 1933 edition of *The Poet C. P. Cavafy*. Malanos shows that Cavafy retained an ambiguity in gender throughout his first-person erotic poems, and though the homosexual context of the poetry in the third person becomes unmistakable with the poet's growing candor, it is usually by analogy to these poems rather than by direct identification of the love involved that the reader of the Greek text comes to see the first-person/second-person poems as part of the same world inhabited by the male homosexual protagonists portrayed through narrative or description in the third person. Without the advantage of George Savidis' chronological tables of composition and publication (in *Unpublished Poems*) and without a knowledge of Cavafy's unpublished work, Malanos' outline of the revelation is rather inaccurate, and the conclusions he draws from it sometimes misdirected, for example, the several irrelevant hypotheses he offers to explain Cavafy's change from silence to progressive candor: the increasingly tolerant post-World War I years (the revelation begins in 1912-13, and the context becomes clear within a few years thereafter; in this connection Savidis suggests [*The Editions of Cavafy*, p. 195] that "a significant contributing factor to the poet's decision to present in public, finally, the erotic facet of his work must have been the favorable climate that had come to prevail in Alexandria a year earlier [i.e., 1911] when the most progressive group on the editorial board of the journal *Nea Zoe* broke away from their colleagues and established a journal of their own called *Grammata*, basing their action on the refusal of the other board members to publish a 'daring' poem by Varnalis: 'Sacrifice' "), the poet's age (presumably so advanced as to permit reckless honesty), and "just maybe the fact that, as of a certain period, he was no longer an employee" (Cavafy retired in 1922, eighteen years after he wrote "On the Stairs" and "At the Theatre," and ten years after the published revelation begins).

4. Dates following the titles of poems quoted in this chapter refer to dates of composition as designated by George Savidis in the tables mentioned in note 3 or in the notes to *Collected Poems*. This applies to poems written through 1925. Thereafter, the dates offered are those of first publication, because Cavafy ceased to record dates of composition after 1925.

5. Malanos's evident distaste for homosexual revelations in general ("The anomalous person who wants to confess all aspects of his life will rarely escape the ridiculous" [*The Poet C. P. Cavafy*, p. 102]) apparently moves him to suggest that Cavafy's principal motive for offering a detailed and continuing revelation was to demonstrate that the tribula-

tions of a homosexual are equal to those of a heterosexual: "Indeed, his manner of presenting it is as though he wanted to say: 'Do you see how many difficulties the life of a pervert also holds? Don't think it's all exclusively yours. Here's a picture of his life, and here's another, and another . . . ' " (p. 104). He sees the poet "monotonously chewing over the confession of his perversion" (p. 101), and he concludes that "Cavafy's poetry, in my opinion, flourishes so long as fear (brought on by society's censorship) strengthens his inventiveness, and declines so long as this fear slackens" (p. 102), a conclusion that leads him to prefer Cavafy's early "symboliste" efforts to the mature erotic poems of the revelation.

6. See Savidis, *The Editions of Cavafy*, pp. 192 ff.

7. The Eliot quotation, from his now famous review of *Ulysses*, first appeared in *The Dial*, November, 1923, p. 483, and has been frequently quoted in secondary sources since. The Joyce phrase, which he indicates Eliot devised in conversation, appears in a letter to Harriet Weaver, November 19, 1923 (see Richard Ellmann, *James Joyce*, p. 541 and fn. 3).

8. The earliest versions of "One of Their Gods" (1899) and "Craftsman of Wine Bowls" (1903), however, very likely had an erotic dimension similar to that of the published versions, and "Growing in Spirit" (1903) includes what the turn of the century might have taken for a rather avant garde line: "Sensual pleasure will have much to teach him."

9. In the note to "September, 1903" that appeared in *Passions and Ancient Days* (p. 63), Cavafy tells us that the first two of these "were really written in October and December 1903, but were perfected and catalogued in January 1904." The manuscript bears the initials "A. M.," which almost certainly refer to a minor Athenian poet of those years, Aleco Mavroudis, whom Cavafy probably met during his second visit to Athens, from August to October of 1903.

10. In *Justine*.

11. My source for the character of Cavafy's neighborhood in those years is Mr. Basil Athanassopoulos, who was among the group of young men of letters who sometimes met with Cavafy at his home in the Rue Lepsius to discuss literary matters and who was kind enough to escort me on a tour of that area and others relating to Cavafy during my visit to Alexandria in March, 1973. I am also grateful to Stratis Tsirkas and Robert Liddell for patiently sharing their knowledge of the city and relevant aspects of Cavafy's biography. The biographical details and the quotations from Cavafy, several published originally in other sources, appear in Mr. Liddell's *Cavafy*.

12. Some of the commentary on this poem and the one that follows first appeared in the introduction to *Passions and Ancient Days*.

13. *On the Greek Style*, p. 157.

14. As George Savidis once pointed out in conversation, the fact that the name Alexandria appears only in "Days of 1909, '10, and '11" among the contemporary erotic poems (and even here with reference to ancient Alexandria) suggests that Cavafy was fully aware of the poetic,

even "mythical", element in his re-creation of modern Alexandria, and that he intended his image of the contemporary city to carry general, symbolic connotations outside a specific geography: those connotations that I have attempted to highlight in the phrase chosen for the title of this chapter.

15. Since the poets of the Greek anthology (followed by the rather different perspectives of Catullus and Martial), there is hardly anything that seems appropriate for comparison; and the generally vague, indirect eroticism of Whitman and Wilde bears only a slight resemblance to what Cavafy was attempting to do.

Chapter 4: Mythical Alexandria

1. G. Lechonitis reports that Cavafy once said: "As a general rule great writers and poets wrote their best work while young, before reaching old age. I am a poet of old age. The more lively events don't inspire me right away. It's first necessary for time to pass. I recall them later and am inspired." (*Cavafian Self-comments*, p. 21). George Seferis suggests one possible effect of Cavafy's late ripening and of his unhurried attitude toward his poetic development: "In the poems of his youth and even certain poems of his middle age he quite often appears ordinary and lacking in any great distinction. But in the poems of old age he gives the impression that he is constantly discovering things that are new and very valuable . . . . It is a strange and rare thing: he died at seventy, but he left us with the bitter curiosity we feel about a man who has been lost to us in the prime of life." (*On the Greek Style*, p. 121-122)

2. Francis Golffing in his provocative—if sometimes abstract—essay based on attitudes in Cavafy, "The Alexandrian Mind: Notes Toward a Definition," p. 76.

3. I indicated above (chapter 3, note 2) that the term "historical" was one of three Cavafy himself used to designate the major categories of his work, the other two being "philosophical" and "erotic." Such general designations tend to be restrictive—especially in the case of Cavafy, where all three categories can be found in the same poem and where there are at least two kinds of historical poems—those specifying a historical date and those having no stated date—but the poet's use of this shorthand term may legitimize our use of it here. An interesting aspect of the so-called historical poems is the manner in which they sometimes manipulate and fictionalize history for the purpose of shaping a mythology, one theme of our exploration in this chapter.

4. During this period, a number of poems were published the year they were written, but some poems were not published for a year or two, and one poem ("If Actually Dead") was not published for as long as ten years after composition. Since Cavafy's development in style and method had reached a relatively stable plateau by 1911, and since the primary concern of this chapter is to characterize the image of ancient Alexandria that Cavafy gradually projected in the work he distributed to his readers during these years, the dates given in parentheses beside the titles of poems will be those of publication rather than composition.

5. See p. 19.

6. As the Greek language is described in the late poem, "In a Township of Asia Minor."

7. The character of the life revealed in "For Ammonis, Who Died at 29, in 610" would seem to qualify the conclusion that Peter Bien draws at one point in his generally excellent introductory monograph on the Greek poet, *Constantine Cavafy*. Bien suggests (on pp. 30-31) that Cavafy's "historical survey of Alexandria" terminates with "If Dead Indeed" (or "If Actually Dead"), a poem that evokes Alexandria under the Emperor Justin I, 518-527 A.D., when, according to the poem, the city had become "godly," and in its piety "detested pitiful idolators." Bien goes on to conclude that this poem, with what he calls "its bitterly ironic conclusion," brings to an end "a survey which has taken us from the glories of the initial Ptolemies in the third century B.C." through eight centuries of a changing history to this last "dismal period [i.e., the early sixth century] when, with Christianity the compulsory religion," glorious Alexandria "was no more." The glories of the Ptolemies were indeed no more, and the influence of Hellenism was no longer central; but clearly the principal mode of life in Cavafy's mythical city, with its devotion to beautiful young men, hedonism, art, and the Greek language, managed to survive the changing pattern of history from Ptolemaic times through at least the death of Ammonis in the early seventh century, almost a hundred years after Justin's reign, when we find Egyptians—including Christian Copts—depicted by Cavafy as having adjusted to Christianity with sufficient cunning to celebrate a life—"our life"—as characteristic of Cavafy's image as any of those lives belonging to earlier centuries, even if the participants are no longer Greek. Cavafy's image is one of tenacity and flexibility: the capacity of those living his kind of Alexandrian life to survive—in some measure and some form—the changing influences of history, including the instrusion of pious and intolerant regimes, whether under a pagan such as Julian or a Christian such as Justin—that is, until the cataclysmic intrusion of Islam gradually snuffs out all but the few lingering remnants of Hellenic culture that we find in "Exiles," circa A.D. 870. This aspect of Cavafy's conception is explored more fully in chapter 5.

8. See *Life of Antony*, par. 54.

9. As was pointed out by C. M. Bowra in "Constantine Cavafy and the Greek Past," in *The Creative Experiment*, p. 40.

10. *The Poet C. P. Cavafy*, p. 312, and *Cavafian Self-comments*, pp. 31-32.

11. The significance of Cavafy's progress from Caesar's predicament to the possible fate of the reader's neighbor and—by sympathy, proximity, and shared destiny—to that of the reader himself, for the purpose of establishing the contemporaneity of his historical "lesson", apparently escapes Malanos, who questions the role of the "you" in this poem: " . . . if this prosaic man, humble and quiet, never worried about eminence, I don't understand for what possible reason he too has to concern himself with the inner voice of conscience that, perhaps justly, at the same time poisons the happiness of his neighbor" (*The Poet C. P. Cavafy*, p. 313). The point of the second stanza is that those without the eminence of Caesar, those who have never aspired to more than what

their quiet, regulated, prosaic lives offer, are still open to a vision of sudden horror entering their neighbor's house, or, perhaps, even their own. The second stanza does not ask whether this horror is a just or unjust visitation or even a matter of "inner conscience." It is a statement against complacency and, even more important, a dramatic evocation of the unexpected horror that may lie in wait for anyone, as the poet himself suggests in his note: "The symbol (Julius Caesar) is found in the first part of the poem; the poet leaves him behind in the second part, where he addresses everybody." (See note 10, above.)

12. One feels called on to take some exception to the characterization of Cavafy's generic hero offered by Edmund Keeley and Philip Sherrard in the introduction to their *Six Poets of Modern Greece* and to the related characterization that appeared in Sherrard's *The Marble Threshing Floor*. The generic hero outlined in these sources reveals almost none of the redeeming attributes of the figure Cavafy actually projects —for example, his measure of courage, pride, self-awareness, shrewdness, and fortitude—while the outline emphasizes too heavily (and perhaps too unsympathetically) what is described as the hero's selfishness, absurdity, depravity, and fatigue, his aging into impotence and ugliness, his sentimentality, nostalgia, and dread of death. This characterization of the generic hero seems to draw in large part on those poems dominated by Cavafy's hedonistic/artistic bias, without sufficient regard for the more complicated (and less negative) image that emerges from the poet's treatment of Greek politics and history—an image explored more fully in chapters 5 and 6.

Chapter 5: The World of Hellenism

1. Dates in parentheses are those of first publication. The full text of "Philhellene" is quoted in chapter 2.

2. I am grateful to Peter Mackridge for suggesting that the speaker in "Philhellene" has some awareness of the world he lives in, for all his barbarian pretension.

3. The remark was made to Stratis Tsirkas in conversation and was first reported by Timos Malanos in *About Cavafy*, p. 56.

4. *Two Cheers for Democracy*, pp. 249-250.

5. Osroini was a kingdom in Mesopotamia, east of northern Syria.

6. The poem, written in 1906, is among the important "unpublished" works that Cavafy did not print during his lifetime.

7. In the Introduction to *Passions and Ancient Days*. Of course "Poseidonians" did not appear in print until some years after Forster's estimate.

8. The region covered the west coast of Asia Minor from Smyrna to Miletus and included the adjacent islands. It was largely here that early Greek literature and philosophy developed.

9. Written in 1913. The title in the original is "Ἔτσι": "so" or "thus".

10. Of the various Hellenistic cities that bore the name, one of the several in Syria would seem to be indicated since the poet uses the phrase "a Greek from Syria or a stranger," which suggests that a Greek

from Syria is not a stranger to the citizens of Selefkia. Of the Syrian cities so named, Selefkia Pieria, so close to Cavafy's favorite Syrian city, Antioch, would seem the likeliest guess, but only a guess in view of the poet's deliberate lack of specificity.

11. G. Valeta was perhaps the first to underline Cavafy's enthusiasm for Antioch after 1917 ("Cavafy the Antiochian," pp. 222-225), though he exaggerates the difference and slights the similarity between Cavafy's images of the two cities, calling Alexandria Cavafy's "mother" and Antioch his "mistress," the former primarily a source of wisdom, the latter of joy. Such a distinction might cause Cavafy's Iasis to smile rather grimly from his grave: " . . . Traveler, / if you're an Alexandrian, you won't blame me. / You know the pace of our life—its fever, its absolute devotion to pleasure."

12. A. A. Vasiliev, *History of the Byzantine Empire*, vol. 1., p. 73.

13. *The Works of the Emperor Julian*, vol. 2, pp. 423 and 425. I am indebted for this quotation and the evidence it offers about Julian's satirical mode to a paper on Cavafy's Julian poems submitted by Pamela Sharpless to Professor George Savidis' course in Modern Greek Poetry at the College Year in Athens.

14. As Cedric Whitman has pointed out to me, it can be said that Cavafy's figure of Julian is another example of phony Hellenism that extends the images offered by "A Prince from Western Libya" and the "philhellenic" monarch from beyond Phraata, in this instance a reactionary, pedantic, dull form of Hellenism that did not progress beyond the resurrection of dead forms.

15. The full implications of this poem are discussed in chapter 6.

16. Seferis—whose commentary on the poem (*Essays*, vol. 1, pp. 441-447) includes a monologue by Aeschylus answering the charge implicit in the vivacious young man's exhortation—appears to be disturbed by his sense that the poet may be saying: "Look how these young men are behaving" and a conflicting sense that Cavafy shares the vivacious young man's sentiments regarding poetic commitment. Seferis more or less settles the question by indicating that the inclusion of these sentiments diminishes the poem. But one could argue that it is this very ambiguity that adds subtlety to the poem.

17. For a fuller discussion of this poem, see chapter 6.

18. There is no precise evidence as to when the final draft of this poem was written, but some time after 1914 seems likely (see the note to the poem in *Collected Poems*). Theophilos Palaiologos—grammarian, mathematician, and humanist—was kinsman of the last emperor of Byzantium, Constantine XII Palaiologos. He was killed in the final battle of the Turkish siege of Constantinople in 1453. A second "unpublished" poem focusing on the fall of Constantinople and its treatment in folk songs was written in 1921 under the title "Parthen" (*Unpublished Poems*, pp. 183-184).

Chapter 6: The Universal Perspective

1. *On the Greek Style*, p. 121. See also chapter 4, note 1, of this book.

2. Ibid., p. 125.

3. Ibid., pp. 121-122. In a note that appeared in *Theatro* (Athens, March-April, 1973, p. 12), George Savidis indicates that Cavafy left some 30 "poems in progress" in various stages of completion (few more than "sketches" of poems) in his archives, each such unfinished work kept in a separate folder bearing the title of the poem and a date, presumably of first conception, the dates ranging from May 1918 to April 1932. One of the more finished of these "sketches," entitled "Tigranokerta" and dated May 1929, accompanies the note.

4. "King Claudius," among the unpublished poems, is somewhat longer.

5. As Savidis points out in his note to the poem in *Collected Poems*.

6. As Robert Liddell suggests in *Cavafy: A Critical Biography* (pp. 196-197), Cavafy is not a partisan in matters of religious conflict; he presents both pagan and Christian speakers sympathetically as the dramatic context requires. The poet's own religious persuasion in his late years remained, at least formally, Greek Orthodox. Liddel indicates (p. 205) that "What or how much Cavafy himself believed we hardly know; we are told that he always wore a cross around his neck . . . . We know that on Good Fridays he used to wait in the street, hat in hand, for the emergence of the beautiful and touching funeral procession of Christ from the patriarchate. We do not know if this was only a love of Greek forms, or if he had any religious conviction." And Liddell also reports (p. 206) that when the patriarch came to the hospital to visit the poet on his deathbed, Cavafy "at first refused to see him, for the visit had been arranged without his knowledge; then he consented, and apparently received the last sacraments with contrition." For further commentary on Cavafy's Christianity as seen from two still different perspectives, see G. P. Savidis, "Was Cavafy a Christian?" in his collection of essays *Pano Nera*, and George Seferis, *A Poet's Journal: Days of 1945-1951*, p. 141. But however we may choose to view the poet's personal religious persuasion, what emerges from "Myris" is not a position antagonistic to Christian ritual or favorable to pagan practice, but an evocation once again of an ideology, a commitment to a way of life, that transcends any specific religious conviction or practice, an ideology shared by "the initiated" in Alexandria and elsewhere, whether Jews in A.D. 50, pagans in A.D. 340, Christians under Julian, or Orthodox Greeks in the twentieth century. As we have seen, the tension between this ideology and all others is the occasion for a number of poems during the poet's mature years. Liddell offers a further insight into Cavafy's position regarding "Myris" when he suggests (p. 201) that "In a city of many religions, like Alexandria, Cavafy may have 'verified', indeed have lived this poem, and most painfully. A friend of his once told me that it exactly expressed his own feelings at a Jewish funeral."

7. Jannaios "had eight hundred of the rebels crucified in Jerusalem after their wives and children had been slain before their eyes. The king himself looked on, feasting and taking his ease among his concubines" (F. E. Peters, *The Harvest of Hellenism*, p. 294). The Pharisees, when

Notes to pages 135-143

restored to power by Queen Alexandra after her husband's death in 76 B.C., "took a bloody revenge upon their former tormentors" (p. 295). The phrase by John Mavrogordato appears in a note to his translation of the poem in *The Poems of C. P. Cavafy*, p. 183.

8. G. Lechonitis, *Cavafian Self-comments*, p. 32.

9. See Peters, p. 295.

10. Seferis' commentary on this poem (*On the Greek Style*, pp. 147-149) is very much to the point. He speaks of "the statue that is missing" in the poem. The "pedestal" is "a king and his queen 'successful', 'entirely satisfied', conscious of their power and rank, loyal to their race and creed, proud of having continued the work of their ancestors. Their state is secure; the beautiful procession now going through the streets of Jerusalem is an impressive symbol of sovereignty. Everything is successful, healthy, prosperous." But "the missing statue is Destruction." Seferis elaborates: "Now it is easy to see where the emphasis is in this poem. We have only to look at the repetitions. They highlight two points: the race of Judah and the struggle of the Maccabees to make their country free and independent. These two points mark the deception, for what is happening is just the opposite. The conquest, the great Diaspora, the persecution, the endless agony of the Jews are there, muttering in their sleep, as if dreaming of Alexander Jannaeus and of his Queen and of the great Judas Maccabaeus and his four illustrious brothers, all of whom will dissolve just like dreams as soon as, in a very few years, Destruction awakes." Robert Liddell, after quoting from this elaboration in his biography (p. 198), suggests that "this looks more like a romantic meditation upon a theme from Cavafy than criticism. Cavafy may perhaps have been living for the moment in Jannaeus' day of triumph." To challenge Seferis' argument in this way—especially his insight into "the deception" implicit in the poem's repetitions—is, in my opinion, to miss the point of the poem and to diminish its subtleties.

11. Timos Malanos in *The Poet C. P. Cavafy* (p. 393) identifies the poet and his speaker in a parenthetical comment that sets the tone for his view of the poem: "([so] thinks the character in the poem, and with him, naturally, Cavafy)." Malanos is conscious of the rhetoric in the speaker's description of the great new Hellenic world ("The poet makes us imagine the character ["τύπο"] of this new Greek with, truly, a great deal of skill when, in the fifth stanza of the poem, he employs something that is not his habit: the excited lyricism, the accumulation of adjectives, the phrasing influenced by Asiatic hyperbole"), but Malanos doesn't explore further the implications of these rhetorical flourishes, and his view of the poem allows no room for irony or ambiguity. He also asks why the poet situated his speaker in 200 B.C., but his answer again doesn't carry through to the full implication: "I think there is no other reason but that this date lies between a new high point of Hellenism (marked by the dates 212-204 B.C.) and the beginning of its decline (marked by the total destruction at Magnesia in 190 B.C.)." But Malanos' notes on specific poems in the fourth section of his book—especially those relating to historical poems—are generally valuable for the

student of Cavafy's work, and given the fact that they were originally published in 1943, they should be regarded as a pioneer enterprise.

12. The line in Greek has a colloquial tone that frustrates precise translation: "Γιὰ Λακεδαιμονίους νὰ μιλοῦμε τώρα!"

13. Cavafy's deliberately planned, gradual revelation of his erotic preoccupations, his frequent revision and re-arrangement of his work, and the continuing control he exercised over its distribution suggest that he was unusually self-conscious about the progress of his work and about the particular pattern he wished it to assume for his select group of readers. But whatever the poet's own sense of the direction his work was taking over the years—and there is little logical reason to think that a creator with Cavafy's kind of aesthetic perfectionism and critical intelligence was unaware of what he was creating—the reader of his work benefits by discerning and accommodating the unifying element, the unifying mythology, that relates one poem to another. As his fellow poet Seferis puts it, "the work of Cavafy should be read and judged not as a series of separate poems, but as one and the same poem . . . . Cavafy is, I think, the most 'difficult' poet of contemporary Greece, and we shall understand him more easily if we read him with the feeling of the continuous presence of his work as a whole" (*On the Greek Style*, p. 125). We get an insight into Cavafy's own keen awareness of pattern in his work from a note that appeared in the May 1927 issue of *Alexandrini Techni*, a journal described by Savidis (*Cavafy Editions*, p. 209) as "Cavafy's personal organ, which provided many such notes that comment on his work, notes that were apparently dictated and checked —if not actually written—by the poet himself" [a note with corrections in the poet's hand survives]. The May 1927 note (quoted by Savidis, pp. 209 ff.), though unsigned as usual, seems to speak with the authority of the poet behind it, and even if the tone appears at moments rather uncharitable toward one of his important early critics, it is perhaps worth our offering a full translation of the note for the purposes of our argument here:

Now let us say a few things about the brief article by Mr. Malanos that appeared in the bulletin *Notes*. It is evidence of his incapacity to understand the spirit of Cavafy's poetry. He lacks a knowledge of Cavafy's poetics.

Cavafy never repeats himself.

Simply look at the pattern that emerges to date from his work.

He has three areas of concern: the philosophical, the historical, and the erotic (or sensual).

The historical area sometimes touches so nearly on the erotic (or sensual) that it is difficult for one to classify some of the poems in these areas. Difficult: not impossible. Of course this would not be work for someone as inexperienced in criticism as Mr. Malanos.

One never finds repetition in Cavafy. Each of his poems, without exception, offers something different from all the others. This, as is well known, is one of the *primary rules* of composition in Cavafy. Each new poem adds something (sometimes a lot, sometimes a little) to one of the three areas mentioned above. Sometimes poems are added to an area to supplement it. Sometimes the light of a new poem subtly penetrates the half-light of an older poem (light in one poem, half-light in the other—not haphazardly, but with great attention to poetic balance).

There is no repetition in Cavafy—rather, there is a return to one of his three areas of concern (one of his thematic categories). Only a novice in criticism such as Mr. Malanos could misunderstand this. Cavafy, powerful craftsman that he is, knows the areas in which he has the capacity to work, and he remains within their boundaries; within these and these alone; and rightly so.

14. The Eliot quotation is from "What Is Minor Poetry?" p. 44.
15. *On the Greek Style*, p. 125.

Index of Poems by Cavafy

General Index

Lechonitis, G, 21, 97, 180n1
Lefkios, 82, 90
Libya, 77; Kyrini, 115
Liddell, Robert, 8, 11, 152, 173n3, 179n11, 184n6, 185n10
London: in 1907 note, 19, 23
Longinus, 92

Maccabaios (Maccabaeus), Judas, 142, 185n10
Maccabees, 142, 185n10
Macedonians, 109
Mackridge, Peter, 182n2
Magnesia, battle of, 115, 123, 147, 185n11
Malanos, Timos, 46, 97, 175n2, 178n3, 178n5, 181n11, 185n11, 186n13
Martial, 69, 180n15
Mavrogordato, John, 143, 185n7
Mavroudis, Aleco, 179n9
Mebis: in "Sophist Leaving Syria," 117; in "Simeon," 126
Media, 106, 109
Meleager, 125
Myrtias, 90, 102
"Mythical method," 46

Narrations, 17n, 31, 37, 40
Nasser, Gamal Abdel, 5, 71
Nea Zoe, 10, 22, 178n3
Nicomedia, 115
Nile River, 118
Nonnos, 88
Notes (periodical), 186n13

Octavian, 96
Origen, 92
Orophernis, 114

Paganism: under Julian, 121; in conflict with Christianity, 136-38
Palaiologos, Theophilos, 130, 183n18
Palamas, Kostis, 11
Pangalos, Theodore, 11
Pathetic fallacy, 140
Peloponnese, 34
Perseus, king of Macedonia, 123
Persia, 34, 115
Persians, 126
Petridis, Pavlos, 22
Pharisees, 143
Pharsalus, 97
Philhellenes, 109

Philip V of Macedonia, 123, 124, 147
Phraata, 106
Pinchin, Jane, 173n3
Plato's Charmidis, 110
Plotinus, 92
Plutarch, 6, 77, 94
Pompey, 97, 143
Pound, Ezra, 7, 46, 100, 151
Poseidonia (Paestum), 111
Poseidonians, 34
Proteus, 56, 57, 63
Proust, Marcel, 151
Ptolemy I Soter, 79
Ptolemy III, 127, 144
Ptolemy IV, 128, 145
Ptolemy VI Philometer, 98, 99
Ptolemy VIII Evergetis, 98
Pydna, battle of, 123

Quartier Attarine, 8, 49, 51, 52

Rallis, Mikes, 18
Raphael: in "For Ammonis . . .," 83, 89, 90, 101
Remon, 110
Rhianos, 125
Rhyme in Cavafy, 16n-17n
Romans, 94, 111, 124; their supremacy in the East, 147
Roman Senate, 98
Romantic imagery, 24
Rome, 34, 94, 98, 123, 124
Rue Cherif Pacha, 3
Rue Lepsius, 5, 10, 20, 52
Rue Rosette, 4
Rue Sharm el Sheikh, 5
Ruskin, John, 33

Sakkas (Saccas), 91, 92; pupil of, 94, 95, 117, 119
Savidis, George, 17n, 20, 22, 146, 175n2, 175n9, 178n3, 179n14, 184n3, 184n6, 186n13
Seferis, George, 7, 12, 24, 45, 56, 63, 100, 126, 135, 152, 175n2, 176n16, 177n24, 180n1, 183n16, 184n6, 185n10, 186n13
Selefkia (Seleucia), 12, 34, 49, 107, 113, 130, 183n10
Selefkides (son of Selefkos), 79, 93
Selefkidis, Dimitrios (Dimitrios Sotir), king of Syria, 98, 124
Selefkids, 142, 143
Shakespeare, William, 6, 77, 176n17

R01 0222 2577

in BCL³

R01 0222 2577   889.
                                109
                                C31K

KEE

CAV
Y

HAR
CH

77-007593-5   889.
         9.00   109
                                C31K
         Houston Public Library
KEELEY, EDMUND
         CAVAFYS ALEXANDRIA
STUDY OF A MYTH IN
PROGRESS

3

                                889.
77-007593-5   109
                                C31K

HOUSTON PUBLIC LIBRARY

CENTRAL LIBRARY
500 MCKINNEY